# The Garden of Eloquence

Books by Willard R. Espy

Bold New Program
The Game of Words
Omak Me Yours Tonight
Oysterville: Roads to Grandpa's Village
An Almanac of Words at Play
Another Almanac of Words at Play
A Children's Almanac of Words at Play
The Life and Works of Mr. Anonymous
O Thou Improper, Thou Uncommon Noun
Say It My Way
Have a Word on Me
Espygrams
The Garden of Eloquence

# The Garden of Eloquence

## A RHETORICAL BESTIARY

### WILLARD R. ESPY
Drawings by Teresa Peekema Allen

Including portions of the first
*Garden of Eloquence*
Published in 1577
by HENRY PEACHAM

*1817*

HARPER & ROW, PUBLISHERS, New York
Cambridge, Philadelphia, San Francisco,
London, Mexico City, São Paulo, Sydney

Special thanks to Dmitri Borgmann, Mary J. Hazard, Darryl Francis, Ralph Beaman, and A. Ross Eckler for their valuable contributions which originally appeared in *Word Ways* published by A. Ross Eckler.

Grateful acknowledgment is made for permission to reprint:

Excerpts from *Verbatim, The Language Quarterly.*
Specified material from p. 80 in *Amadeus,* a play by Peter Schaffer. Copyright © 1980, 1981 by Peter Schaffer. By permission of Harper & Row, Publishers, Inc., and The Lantz Office, Inc.
CAUTION! *Amadeus* is the sole property of the author and is fully protected by copyright. All rights, including professional, amateur, motion picture, recitation, lecturing, public reading, radio broadcasting and the rights of translating into foreign languages, are strictly reserved. All inquiries should be addressed to the author's agents: The Lantz Office, Inc., 888 Seventh Avenue, New York, N.Y. 10106.

FIRST EDITION

*Designer: Abigail Sturges*

---

Library of Congress Cataloging in Publication Data

Espy, Willard R.
   The Garden of Eloquence.

   "Includes portions of the first Garden of Eloquence
published in 1577 by Henry Peacham."
   1. Figures of speech—Dictionaries.   I. Peacham,
Henry, 1546–1634. Garden of Eloquence. Selections.
1983.   II. Title.
PN227.E84   1983      808'.003       83–47530
ISBN 0–06–181256–0

---

83 84 85 86 87 10 9 8 7 6 5 4 3 2 1

# CONTENTS

# ACKNOWLEDGMENTS

WHILE the principal source of the material in this bestiary is the Reverend Henry Peacham himself, I have made wide use of other references, particularly for modern examples of rhetorical devices. I have drawn liberally on *Word Ways* and *Verbatim*, two magazines on words that are entirely different but equally delightful, and I wish to acknowledge my indebtedness to their respective editors, A. Ross Eckler and Laurence Urdang, both of whom I am proud to consider as friends. My thanks to Steele Commager, who provided the most likely pronunciations for the rhetorical devices that populate this book. It was no mean service, since in most instances the stress changed when a Greek word entered Latin, and changed again when it became English. I have never met N. H., S. K., or P. S. Mager, authors of *Power Writing, Power Speaking* (New York: William Morrow, 1978), but I hope to; their collection of present-day twists of rhetoric is superb, and I have frequently borrowed examples from it when I could not find others as good. A very special nod to David Pearce, who years ago sent me a book on rhetoric that triggered the one you are about to read. To these, and to all the others who have contributed knowingly or unknowingly to this book, my very hearty thanks.

By the great might of figures (which is no other thing than wisdom speaking eloquently), the orator may lead his hearers which way he lists, and draw them to what affection he will; he may make them to be angry, to be pleased, to laugh, to weep, and lament; to love, to abhor, and loathe; to hope, to fear, to covet; to be satisfied, to envy, to have pity and compassion; to marvel, to believe, to repent; and briefly to be moved with any affection that shall serve best for his purpose.

—Henry Peacham
*The Garden of Eloquence*

# The Garden of Eloquence

# INTRODUCTION

**Rhet o ric**   RET uh rik   *n*. (Gr. *rhetor*, orator).
1. The art of expressive speech or of discourse, esp. of literary composition.
. . . Originally, as cultivated by the Greeks, the study of the principles and
technical resources of oratory, including both composition and delivery.
. . . Now, esp., the art of writing well in prose . . . 2. Hence: *a*. Skillful or
artistic use of speech; skill in the effective use of speech. *b*. Artificial elegance
of language, or declamation without conviction or earnest feeling.—*Webster's
New International Dictionary,* Second Edition

THE purpose of this book, to the extent that it has a serious purpose, is
to encourage the rehabilitation of rhetoric, a language asset that we have
consigned to outer darkness for two hundred years.

The current reputation of rhetoric is dismal. On the one hand it is
reproached as vulgar ostentation. On the other hand it is equated with
deceit, if not downright wickedness.

Our suspicion of rhetoric extends even to its lovely offspring, eloquence. Rhetoric and eloquence make us nervous because we sense in
them a terrible power. We know that the ends of power can as easily be
evil as good, and we are frightened in our hearts. Granted that the
eloquence of a Jesus Christ set for mankind a goal of goodness and love
to which we still aspire; yet it must be granted also that the eloquence of
an Adolf Hitler led a great nation into madness, and forced a great
civilization to the edge of destruction.

Scorn is a common cover for fear, and it is fashionable to scorn
rhetoric, though we know perfectly well that good or evil is no more
inherent in it than in a thundercloud or in the energy of the atom. The
good and evil are in ourselves.

So I suggest that we first apologize to rhetoric for the rude treatment we have accorded it, and then ask it to come back to work for us. We need it.

Rhetoric offers as fresh and exciting an approach to language today as it did when it first made its appearance in Syracuse, a Greek outpost in Sicily, twenty-five hundred years ago. It calls into service the whole network of muscles that articulate the body of language—great muscles for leaping, running, heaving, striking; fine muscles for expanding or contracting the pupil of an eye, or painting a landscape on a canvas smaller than a postage stamp.

If rhetoric were no more than an ornamental contrivance, it would still provide an intellectual and even a sensual pleasure. But far from being merely ornamental, the devices of rhetoric are useful tools. With their aid it is possible to state with force and clarity—yet with all the enhancement of resonance that figures of speech, sentence arrangement, and the rest of rhetoric can supply—what otherwise could be only lamely and partially expressed. Rhetoric is more than a marvelous game. To be sure, anyone who is caught up in a love affair with words will delight aesthetically, regardless of sense, in a thousand rhetorical tricks: in repetition for emphasis, the balance of contrasting ideas in contrasting phrases, and the inversion of sentence order; in abbreviation, irrelevancy, hyperbole, irony, paradox, and climax. There is a sensual fulfillment in metaphor, simile, metonymy, syllepsis, and all their airy kind. But more than that is at stake. Master rhetoric, and you have mastered persuasion. Persuade, and you have gone a long way toward mastering your social environment.

The definition of a rhetorical term may vary so from one authority to another that one wonders whether they are both talking about the same word. A single rhetorical device, on the other hand, may travel under several names. The names and definitions in this book are the ones I happen to prefer.

Rhetoric came into being to meet a practical need. In 466 B.C., the citizens of Syracuse unseated their ruler and called home a horde of exiles, who promptly filed lawsuits to regain property that the state had seized from them. Being frequently weak on documentary support for their claims, the plaintiffs were forced to turn to reasoning from inference; and a scholar named Corax told them how to go about it. Divide your speeches, he said, into four parts: a short preface; narrative arguments; related remarks; and a peroration. Substitute general probability where you lack hard evidence. If, for illustration, a puny man is accused of assaulting a large one, the defendant might well point out the unlikelihood of his attacking a person so superior in strength to himself. A larger man might reply to the same charge, "Is it plausible that I should have committed an assault where the presumption was sure to be against me?"

A century and a half later, Aristotle wrote *Rhetoric,* the first detailed analysis of the art of persuasion—for art it is, he insisted, since a speaker, to persuade, must use tools that can be identified. He assigned rhetoric to the branch of art known as popular logic; its aim must be not simply to excite emotions, but to prove a point, or at least give the appearance of proving it. The charge that rhetoric has no concern over right or wrong, but wishes merely to persuade for the love of persuasion, has bedevilled it ever since.

The Roman orator Cicero, however, added a moral dimension: The perfect orator, he held, is the perfect man, ripe in virtue no less than in logic.

As the purity of the early art yielded increasingly to forced conceits, rhetoric was gradually demeaned and set aside; by the time of the Middle Ages, few traces of it remained. It re-emerged with the Renaissance and the revival of learning, only to fade once more in the eighteenth century. Today the word *rhetoric* has become pejorative. "That's just rhetoric," we say, meaning: "That's just hot air."

It is high time to reassess the merits of this marvelous instrument. I venture this notion because it seems to me that interest in the pleasures and practicalities of language has burgeoned over the past ten years or so—that is, since the period 1970–75. A multiplied audience is consuming a multiplied supply of articles and books that deal with words—word play, word analysis, word origins; usage, semantics, linguistics. This may be only a fad, and there is little evidence that it reflects a general rise in the quality of written or spoken English; still, it is good news.

The interest is not simply elitist. My own mail regularly includes— among letters from men and women with professional ties to language —pungent and sometimes wonderfully witty offerings from correspondents who boast that they never finished high school, and from children whose high school days still lie ahead.

However brief this burgeoning may prove, it provides a fine opportunity to take another look at the pleasures and practicalities of rhetoric. Remember, you need not use it to cheat your neighbor; it works just as well if you are trying to help him. Quite apart from the morals of the matter, you will find that rhetoric is great fun. And quite apart from its being fun, it has such side benefits as shining up your conversational and writing skills.

Now there's no harm in that, is there?

# WIND
# FROM THE WEST

F you had seen Louise on hands and knees in the front yard this morning, weeding the York roses, or me cleaning the ashes from the fireplace and exiling the fire tongs and poker and bellows to the shed, you would have known that summer had arrived at last in Oysterville. And if you had seen me a little later lying in the sun on the deck behind the Red Cottage, you would have known how I put my summers to use.

Not that I was napping. No; I was improving my mind. I was reading a book written more than four hundred years ago by a minister named Henry Peacham (sometimes he spelled it Pecham). The book is a course in tricks of magic—not sleight of hand, but sleight of words. The Reverend Peacham's intent was to turn his readers into "most eloquent poets and orators"; and while I have long since lost hope of becoming a most eloquent poet or orator, I still entertain fantasies of smoothing out my writing. So I opened *The Garden of Eloquence* as eagerly as someone else might investigate a book that promises to salt and pepper sex relations, or to trim bodies at no price of diet and exercise, or to make millionaires at no risk, money refunded promptly if not completely satisfied.

When I was well into my reading, the breeze against my face freshened; the alder trees at the west side of the yard began to sigh, and a door slammed in Michael Parker's house, a hundred feet to the south. My ear pricked at this because I knew the house to be empty and locked; Michael began building it awhile back, but for some reason stopped just before it was finished; no one has visited it in six months. An open door might mean a break-in. I walked over to check.

The near door was the one slamming. I stepped inside to see if anything appeared out of the way. Michael's house is almost as small as

Chris Freshley's (which lies two hundred feet to the west) or my own—you never saw three homes more compact than ours. It took only moments to investigate the living room and kitchen on the ground floor and the bedroom and bath upstairs, and I found no signs of disturbance. But there was something odd about the kitchen.

Michael had set a window in the west wall, so that a person washing dishes could look west to Chris's house and the alder and spruce woods behind it. But the sink was still to be installed—and the window was no longer there. Where it should have been were a pair of french doors that certainly had not been around before.

They were unlocked. I pushed them open, and stepped outside.

Michael's place was gone. So was Chris's. So was mine. I was standing between two ranks of white Doric columns, made of wood, on a balcony, looking down a row of white steps to . . . but at sight of what the steps led down to, I panicked; my eyes snapped shut; my hands clenched into fists; even the toes of my feet tried to clench. Shudders racked me, and my breath, or what remained of it, came and went in gasps. I cannot guess how long it was before the clenching and quivering and gasping subsided enough so that I could turn to flee back home.

When at last I did turn, and dared to open my eyes, I found myself facing the white clapboarded wall of a three-story house. Tightly drawn white shutters blinded the rows of windows. Where Michael's french doors had been there now stood a white door whose top edge I could not have touched at the uppermost limit of the reach of my hand, and it was proportionately wide. The knocker and the doorknob, both of a pale yellow metal, were as outsized as the door, and as high in scale; the knocker was at the level of my chin, and the knob but little lower.

I hurried over and grasped the knob; it would not turn. I took the knocker in both hands and pounded, using all my force; when I paused to listen, there was only silence inside the house. I pounded again, listened again; this time I made out an approaching tread, slow, heavy, ominous, and as deliberate as the ticking of the grandfather's clock in my living room. I shall hear that tread in my nightmares until the day I die. And as surely as I stood there, I knew that if that great white door swung open I would die indeed.

So I fled the other way—across the balcony, down the white steps three at a time, to meet whatever crouched waiting beyond.

It seems curious now that, though I caught but one appalled glimpse of that landscape when I arrived on the balcony, the nearer details are burned in my memory. It is odd, too, that the sight drove me all but out of my wits with fright; I can attribute such panic only to the shock of stepping without warning into the impossible. For the fact is that the view from the balcony was lovely.

Closest to hand, a hollow square formed by a neatly trimmed laurel hedge enclosed a circle of shrubs, topiarized into spheres, cones, and cubes. At the center of the circle, in a marble basin as large as an average livingroom, a brass Triton lifted above his head a stone dolphin spouting spray. Beyond lay a lawn smoothed out as if for croquet, surrounded by rhododendron bushes ablaze in red, pink, and yellow. The court looked much as I imagine my own croquet garden might if only I could exchange my dandelions, hummocks, indentations, molehills, moss, and yellow patches for impeccable green turf.

West of the croquet court, an orchard of cherry trees flaunted blossoms, as if the season had been spring instead of summer; I was to find later that every bush and tree in the Garden (already I was capitalizing the word in my mind) was either riotous with bloom, if such was its nature, or heavy with ripe fruit.

Still farther west, dwarf hemlocks grew in the shape of a star, with lawn separating the rays; and farther yet I could see a grove of alder trees standing uncomfortably in even rows, like shiny-clean schoolchildren standing to pledge allegiance to the flag when they would much rather be outside playing in the dirt.

I may have made out other details, but the only one I can remember is that gravel paths connected east with west on the borders of all these configurations, and that the paths were lined with pedestals supporting massive blue pots of impatiens—white, pink, rose, lilac, and red.

I had settled for a rocking chair long before jogging became a pervasive disease; my stampede from the white house took me only a few hundred feet up one of the graveled paths before a sharp stitch in my side reminded me that there are more ways than one to die. Looking over my shoulder and seeing no sign of pursuit, I slowed to a walk, and then stopped to catch my breath, making excuses to myself for my cowardice. I could still see the house large behind me, a Georgian mansion so brightly white that it sparkled in the sun. I thought the great door opened a few inches as I watched, but in a moment it closed again.

It was time to rationalize; I seated myself on a green park bench, and began. Doubtless, I reassured myself, this strange Garden was some new enterprise of Chris Freshley, a young Oysterville native who has already chalked up an impressive record as a landscape architect. Admittedly he would have had to proceed with exceptional speed, since there had been no Garden in evidence a few minutes before; but then everyone in Oysterville agrees that Chris is an exceptionally able and fast-working fellow.

Ah well, mysteries exist to be solved. I stood up, drew a long breath, exhaled slowly, and started walking west, away from the mansion, passing the spouting dolphin and the hemlock star and the croquet court and the cherry orchard. Soon I could orient myself only by looking back at the house.

In that one glimpse from the balcony, the landscape had unrolled like a colored relief map, marked out with ponds, bridges, paths, lawns, hedges, groves, and patches of contrasting color. Down here in the midst of it, the relationship between one planting arrangement and another blurred; hedges and trees conspired to cut off my view. When the path took me into the alder grove I lost sight of the white house for good. The path Y'ed, and I took the right-hand branch at random; it Y'd again, and I do not recall which branch I took. Soon I was completely lost. Instead of flower pots, I noticed, the pedestals by the path now held lighthearted statues of piping fawns and dancing nymphs. I left the alder grove, and found the way I had taken was between two privet hedges higher than my head. Once another gravel path crossed mine at right angles, and I saw to left and right still other paths making their way among other hedges; but I passed on, having no wish to be trapped in a maze. When at last the hedges ceased, I found myself crossing a meadow as closely mowed as a putting green; its span must have been a quarter of a mile, and I could not see past the high stone walls on either side. I came to a spruce grove, and paused at a still, dark pool where frogs croaked on lily pads; the pool was fed by a little muttering stream. At another branching I took a way bordered by beds of flowers of different seasons, yet all at the height of their bloom: dahlias, chrysanthemums, cosmos, phlox, roses, spirea, salvia, clematis, marigolds. The flower beds were separated by shrubs, also blooming; I saw hydrangeas, honeysuckle, azaleas, and unfamiliar varieties of rhododendron. The beds were freshly weeded, but there were no gardeners in sight. Yet a spade stood in new-turned earth, and a wheelbarrow loaded with freshly pulled weeds had been left beside a flaming bush clipped to the shape of a ball, and twice as high as a man. Farther on, a coil of red hose was attached to a standing faucet; the spout of the hose dribbled, as if someone had just turned off the faucet. I could see the Garden again to my right and left, each elaborate design cheek by jowl with the next, blocked off finally by fieldstone walls.

The only sound apart from my scuffing on the gravel was that of the wind rustling through the streets. I started to whistle, but broke off, as if it were somehow rude of me to break the silence. Still, I wished a dog would bark, or a crow caw. My heart leaped with relief when at length there broke out behind me a tubercular coughing, of the sort uttered by a reluctant lawn mower when its cord is pulled. I called, "Hello there?" and turned back the way I had come, trotting in eagerness to meet someone. But no one answered, and the coughing sound was not repeated; after a bit I shrugged my shoulders and started west again.

Nothing was quite as it had been moments before.

More earth had been turned by the spade; it stood several feet from its former place. The wheelbarrow was empty of weeds. The hose, uncoiled, was feeding a dribble of water into a clematis bed.

Though I still saw no gardener, I did sense movement just outside the range of my vision. Yet it had to be the creation of nervous imaginings, for when I looked head-on, there was nothing there. Once I fancied that a trowel was at work on its own around a rosebush, and a little later that a rake was assembling cut grass; but trowel and rake were motionless when I focused my gaze.

Then the silence broke. Barely, at first, but with growing loudness, there arose behind me a screeching, as if a fingernail were being drawn endlessly across a blackboard. It was a horrid noise; a cold shiver prickled my spine. In the moment that I hesitated before looking back, the screeching broke into separate parts—scratching, scuttling, slithering. I looked, and shot up the path as if the devil were at my heels.

If not the devil, then near enough. A flood of things that creep and crawl was rushing after me, filling the path as a river in spate fills its banks. There were aphids as large as robins, and cabbage worms, cutworms, and army worms as long as garter snakes. There were earwigs, flea beetles, grasshoppers, mites, mealybugs, pill bugs, sow bugs, snails, slugs, weevils, tent caterpillars, thrips, whiteflies, none smaller than a full-grown rat.

They matched their speed to mine; I could not outrun them. Yet there was a chance that they were going about their own business—that I only happened to be in their way. So I leaped sidewise, handily clearing a bed of phlox; but they veered after me, and the screeching rose in pitch.

In the hurry of events since my arrival at Michael's house there had been no time to notice the slackening of the wind that led me there; but now even in the midst of my terror I gradually realized that it was rising again, blowing hard into my face. It was a gale—no, a tempest—no, a hurricane. Pushing against it, I found myself slowing; running in place; staggering backward. The mightiest blast yet lifted me head over heels and dashed me to the ground. I scrambled groggily to my hands and knees, and looked back.

The wind was hurling my hunters helter-skelter to the east. The larger ones rolled like tumbleweeds along the ground, and the smaller ones spun crazily through the air. In a moment they were gone; and as if at a signal, the wind fell away to a caressing breeze.

Or was it the wind? When I turned the other way I saw leaning over me, puffing softly into my face, a fireplace bellows—the very bellows, I could have sworn from the design of intertwined flowers in the middle of its black cheeks, that I had stowed away in the shed for the summer scarcely an hour before.

And that was only the head of the thing. Its body was a split half of a log, cut to the two-foot length I like for my fires. The arms were undoubtedly my tongs, and my poker was the single leg.

The head expanded and contracted in a metronomic beat, expelling air through its nozzle. The lidless red eyes that had replaced its valves oozed tears.

"Oh, Pops!" sobbed the bellows. "I am so sorry—so dreadfully sorry!"

Pops is not my favorite honorific. "Sorry for what?" I asked, rather peevishly.

"For nearly blowing you away. I thought you were a weed, the way you were leading those dreadful Solecisms against us—you *looked* like a weed—your hair was blowing so—how could I know you weren't a dandelion gone to seed?"

"Don't be ridiculous!" I said. But as I spoke I felt a peculiar sensation, one that I had never experienced before. It was like the first heaven-sent sip of a very dry, very cold martini, along with tantalizing little kisses running down me all the way to my toes. Something was changing in me; the feeling was very pleasant, and very intense, and I wanted it to continue.

"Why, you *are* a dandelion!" the bellows exclaimed in astonishment. "I mean—a *Dandy* Lion!"

And when I looked down at myself, I was.

At least as much of me as I could see was. I was clearly a lion below the neck, though I still stood on only two legs. I felt my tail twitching

behind me; when I told it to swing forward it followed my orders as naturally as any other of my extremities. The tip was a white dandelion puff the size of a tennis ball; but no matter. Blood was pumping handsomely through my veins; I felt like dancing a jig, or turning a somersault, or both.

And my clothes—well! I lacked trousers, to be sure, but who cared? My shirt was a dazzling pink, with scarlet ruffles at the cuff and throat; I wore an elegant sky-blue morning jacket, with buttons that I swear were solid gold; best of all, a yellow sweetheart rose peeped out from my lapel.

I opened my mouth, and roared in sheer delight.

The bellows leaped back a yard and teetered on his single leg. His tears were flowing again.

"Sir Lion—Sir Lion," he sobbed, "don't eat me! I am only wood and iron and leather, Sir Lion—I wouldn't sit well in you at all—"

"I *may* eat you," I said (my voice had gone down an octave) "unless you stop that silly blubbering. And forget that Sir Lion nonsense. I'd rather be Pops."

"Whatever you say, Sir Li—I mean Sir Pops—I mean Pops—"

I spread my lips in what I meant as a kindly smile, but it made him jump back another yard. "The fact is," I said, "that you probably saved my life, and I am very grateful. You almost blew me away, but you did blow away those ghastly things that were after me. Who are you, anyway?"

"Doesn't everybody know, Sir Li—I mean Pops? I am the Gardener. I am very good at blowing things away. Oh dear—you were running from the Solecisms! They have invaded the Garden again! And on Honoring Day, too! Oh dear, oh dear, I must run—I must warn the Queen!"

"Wait a minute," I said. "What do you mean—'I am the Gardener'?"

"I tell the helpers what to weed and spray and mow and sprinkle and fertilize."

"But you are just a hodgepodge of my own fireplace tools! Why, I stored you away in the shed only an hour ago!"

"No; that was four hundred years ago, Pops. The Queen assembled me herself. She said I would make a fine Orator, because I had so much wind."

"Orator?"

"*Everyone* is an Orator in the Garden of Eloquence."

Of course! I had just read in Henry Peacham's book:

I was of a sudden moved to take this Garden in hand, and to set therein such figurative Flowers, both of Grammar and Rhetoric, as do yield the sweet

savor of Eloquence, and to present to the eyes the goodly and beautiful colors of Elocution—such as shine in our speech like the glorious stars in the Firmament; such as beautify it, as flowers of sundry colors—a gallant Garland.

There could be no doubt about it: I was caught in a metaphor.

"So that's it!" I said. "Then you must be a metaphor yourself. But aren't you a very mixed one?"

"I am the way the Queen made me," he replied stiffly. "I am her chief counselor. That should be good enough for you."

"Oh, it is, it is indeed."

But all at once he had forgotten me. His bellows head was cocked as a robin's is when it listens for a worm. His cheeks hesitated in the midst of a contraction. I caught the sound of a bell ringing far to the west.

"Oh, my," wailed the Gardener. "The honoring is about to start! And I am not there to present the Schemes and Tropes to the Queen! And she doesn't know about the invasion! Excuse me, Pops—I must run!"

And run he did, if it be running to charge up a gravel path in great hops on a single leg, as if riding a pogo stick. Yet I easily kept up with him; a lion is never winded. Besides, I had no intention of finding myself alone in the Garden again.

It quickly appeared that there was little chance of that. Traveling at an extraordinary rate, we caught up first with a kangaroo, though he was proceeding in twenty-foot bounds; then a faun, remarkably similar to the statues by the path, pattering along on goat feet and absorbedly playing his pipes; then a white striding stork whose head came to my shoulder. They were all converging on the sound of the bell.

And there were more—I must say, a rum-looking lot. Some were human: a girl in pigtails, on a skateboard; a bent man on roller skates, wearing earphones; a wrinkled biddy, with her white hair blowing out behind her, swinging along on crutches. But most were not human at all.

Among them were animals of all sorts, running some on their two hind legs and some on all four. Several wore snatches of clothing—sports jackets, swim trunks, skirts, bow ties, top hats, sneakers. A wolf with a cub on either shoulder (and four galloping behind) wore a peach-colored, six-cup brassiere. The animals' sizes ran to the mean: the elephants were little taller than the armadillos, and the rabbits scarcely smaller than the sheep.

There were also:

Sphinxes, incubuses, succubuses, phoenixes, griffins;
Elves, trolls, fairies, goblins, giants, and dwarves;
Red devils, and imps with forked tails;
Angels, archangels, cherubim.

There were living artifacts:

Hammers, saws, screwdrivers, pliers, scissors;
Brooms, whisk brooms, mirrors, dustpans, light bulbs, carpet sweepers;
Spoons, forks, dishes, pots, sieves, cups, teakettles, egg beaters, meat grinders;
Pens, pencils, erasers, inkwells, typing paper still in the box;
Baseball bats, tennis racquets, golf sticks, hockey sticks, croquet mallets, pogo mallets, billiard cues, riding saddles;
Rakes, mucking forks, hayforks, shovels, spades, hoses, wheelbarrows, weather vanes, pruning shears, lawn mowers, sprinkling cans, trowels;
And creatures impossible to identify, because they were shifting constantly from one appearance to another.

The clang of the bell was very loud now. We were running up a slope; I marveled that my pulse and respiration remained as placid as if I were strolling about my own yard. At the top of the hill stretched a rail fence, but it was no barrier; the crowd was pouring through an open gate. In a trice, the Gardener and I were through too. As I breasted the hill I saw the sun ahead, hanging halfway down the sky; it had not moved since I left the deck of the Red Cottage.

We had reached our destination—a new-mown, undulating hillside where the hay still lay ungathered, making a natural arena. A grassy aisle divided it into two halves. There was a platform at the bottom, with steps leading up to it. All about me the audience was settling itself as if about to picnic, spreading out blankets and opening hampers of food. The Gardener paused beside me at an empty space, and said, "This should do for you, Pops. I'm sorry I can't stay with you; I have to get down and warn the Queen, you know."

"But what a queer bunch you do have here, to be sure!" I said.

"Not as odd as dandelions gone to seed," he replied. "Just wait for me here, will you, Pops? I'll pick you up after the awards."

With that he pogoed down the aisle and up a set of steps to a stage crowded with a jumble of unfolded folding chairs. Musical instruments lay on some of them, and leaned against others. At the center, a throne of carven oak, its high rounded back surmounted by a wooden crown, dominated the stage. A young woman sat on the throne. The Gardener knelt briefly before her, then stood up and whispered earnestly in her ear.

I could not hear what they were saying, nor did I wish to, for my whole being had surged up to hail the radiance around my Queen. I cannot now for the life of me recall whether her hair was sorrel or auburn or gold, straight or curly or kinky; whether her eyes were oval or round, large or small, blue, green, or brown; whether her nose was straight, or curved, or retroussé; whether her figure was voluptuous or slender. The radiance blurred my vision. I know for sure only that she was beautiful beyond beauty, and—oh, yes—that wings like a butterfly's shimmered on her shoulders.

The Queen waved the Gardener aside, stood, and curtsied to us. I am almost sure that she smiled. Then she sang this rondeau redoublé:

### The Queen of Eloquence to Her Subjects

My rose-crowned children gather at my feet.
    Here, METAPHORUS This to That compares;
Here, wordy PERIPHRASIS takes her seat;
    SYNECDOCHE here Part for Whole declares,

Here Whole for Part; HYPERBOLE outswears
 EXAGGERATIO; here echoes sweet
Form ONOMATOPOEIA's mimicked airs.
 My rose-crowned children gather at my feet.

Here, bracketed PARENTHESIS I meet;
 Here, ZEUGMA merges unalike affairs;
And here's SYLLEPSIS, playful in deceit.
 (Here, METAPHORUS This to That compares.)

Here's PLEONASMUS, glutted with her wares;
 Here, while SARCASMUS utters spiteful bleat,
By opposites IRONIA ensnares.
 (Here, wordy PERIPHRASIS takes her seat.)

METONYMY, by that cold steel he wears,
 Here Warfare shows, and here in bread doth eat
Christ's body. You, my family, my heirs,
 Here come to magnify me.
      (Here I greet
 My rose-crowned children.)

The crowd rose to its many sorts of feet and roared approval. Not just roared; it also brayed, hee-hawed, mooed, mewed, trumpeted, hissed, honked, barked, howled, and chattered.

When at last the Queen could stop curtsying and return to her seat, the orchestra tuned up. There were no musicians; the stringed instruments had their own thin arms to scrape the bows across the strings, and the percussion instruments their own arms to beat with. The wind instruments blew of themselves. And I fell asleep. (The red imp who was seated on the grass next to me told me later that a griffin had nudged a wheelbarrow and whispered, "Look at that old lion. They have just played the opening bar, and he is asleep already.")

A blast of trumpets awakened me. The orchestra had vanished, and the Queen was standing with the Gardener on the platform. She held a wicker basket in one hand.

"Dear workers," she said, "I have upsetting news. The Gardener informs me that the Pests are on the march again. An army of Grammatical Errors attempted an invasion by way of path fourteen a short while ago. Fortunately, he discovered them in time, and was able to blow them away; but we may assume that this was only a reconnaissance party, and that the main force may arrive at any moment. I am therefore issuing a general alert, and must ask that you all, with the exception of those who have been named to receive decorations today, leave this ceremony now and go to your battle stations."

The crowd roared again, and many began making their way uphill to the exit. In a few moments there were scarcely a hundred of us remaining.

# THE FIGURES
# IN THE GARDEN

T HESE ceremonies will be brief," said the Queen, "for we know"—I assumed she was employing the royal "we"— "you would all rather be outside guarding against the enemy than sitting here. If a critical situation develops, word will reach us at once, and we shall dissolve this gathering. But each of you, even the dandelion gone to seed who is the Gardener's guest"—here she looked at me directly for the first time— "have performed services in the upkeep of the Garden that are over and above the call of duty, and we would be delinquent if we failed to express our gratitude. Good Gardener, call the first name."

"ACTIO," shouted the Gardener. A goblin the size of a beach ball bounced to his feet, and went on bouncing until he was down the hill and on the stage beside the Queen. He was making agitated motions—pounding his fist into his palm, winking, scowling, grimacing, shaking hands with himself, throwing his arms up, bumping, grinding, thumbing his nose at the audience, and breathing the while so heavily that he might have been snoring. He managed barely to hold still long enough for the Queen to dip into her basket and bring out a loop of purple ribbon from which was suspended a round mirror in a jeweled brass frame.

In a few words she praised his unstinting service in maintaining the garden, as she was to praise each award winner that followed him; then she slipped over his head and around his shoulders (for as far as I could see, he had no neck) the Medal of the Garden of Eloquence, Third Class.

Actio knelt to the Queen, bounced up, nodded his head, shook it, placed a hand over his mouth, took it away, turned to face the audience, threw back his head, and sang to this effect:

I grant that words do very well, and think it fine to prize them;
   Yet their significance depends on how you *emphasize* them:
   "*He* never claimed you threw that rock" (the claim was made by her);
   "He *never* claimed you threw that rock" (in all his life—no, sir!);
   "He never *claimed* you threw that rock" (a hint is not a claim);
   "He never claimed *you* threw that rock" (he blamed your Auntie Mame);
   "He never claimed you *threw* that rock" (you might have kicked it, too);
   "He never claimed you threw *that* rock" (another rock would do);
   "He never claimed you threw that *rock*" (that cow, perhaps? That weather-
      cock?).

**Actio**   AK tee oh   (L. "driving, doing, action").
The use of stretch, pitch, mimicry, gestures, and the like, to convey
nuances of meaning; delivery.

The written word stands on its own, but the effectiveness of the
spoken word depends on how it is delivered. If you talk through your
nose; if your voice is shrill; if you mumble; if your words fall to the floor
between you and your audience; if you rasp; if you race through your
sentences, or stretch them out to the ends of time—then no matter how
compelling your logic, how elegant your sentence structure, how vivid
your figures of speech, no one will listen.

   Your appearance too—your posture, your dress, your gestures—will
either add to or detract from the force of your words.

   (When I am delivering a talk, one common form of actio is very
noticeable: my knees shake.)

**Tautonym**   TAWT oh nim   (Gr. "identical name").
A taxonomic designation, such as *Gorilla gorilla,* in which the genus
and species name are the same. In rhetoric, any word or name
consisting of two or more identical parts:

   Angang-angang (a kind of Javanese gong)
   Cancan (an exuberant dance)
   Fofofofo (a town in eastern New Guinea)
   Kukukuku (a people inhabiting parts of eastern New Guinea)

## Interminable words

The chemical name for the enzyme tryptophan synthetase A protein consists of 1,913 letters, and there may be other such combinations as long or longer. On page 337 of Liddell & Scott's *Greek Lexicon* there appears a word of 176 letters, meaning "hash."

English is not particularly hospitable to words of inordinate length. We have made a joke of the Latin ablative plural *honorificabilitudinitatibus* (27 letters), meaning "honorableness." The OED accepts the anglicization *honorificabilitudinity* (22 letters), calling it "the very longest word" in our language. (It adds in passing that *straight* and *strength* are the two longest monosyllables.) *Antidisestablishmentarianism* (28 letters) had no separate listing in the OED or Webster's Second.

In some other languages, very long words are more welcome. For instance:

Saint-Remy-en-Bouzemont-Saint-Genest-et-Isson (a town in Quebec): 38 letters.

*Snelpaardelooszonderspoorwegpatrolritjuig* (a Flemish word meaning "a carriage which is worked by means of petroleum, which travels fast, which has no horses, and which is not run on rails"): 41 letters.

Chargoggagoggmanchauggagoggchaubunaqwnaqungamangg (the Algonquin name for a lake in south central Massachusetts—now called Lake Webster—meaning "You fish on your side, I fish on my side, nobody fish in the middle"): 49 letters.

Coeur-Très-Pur-de-la-Très-Bienheureuse-Vierge-Marie-de-Plaisance (unattested; said to be a place in the county of Papineau in Quebec): 54 letters.

Llanfairpwllgwyngyllgogerychwyrndrobwllllantysiliogogogoch (Welsh for "Church of St. Mary in a hollow of white hazel, near to the rapid whirlpool, and to St. Tisilio church, near to a red cave"): 58 letters.

*Gesundheitswiederherstellungsmitterzusammenmischungsuerhaltnisskundinger* (Bismarck's coinage for "apothecary," a word which he considered insufficiently German): 72 letters.

T HERE was a commotion off to my right. Something shouted, "I should have been first! ABBREVIATIO comes before Actio in the alphabet!"

"You are right, old friend," said the Gardener. "Spelling was never my strong point. Do come down."

A creature like a magnified version of those metal jacks that children toss in the game of that name separated from the crowd and rolled down the hill and up the steps. He had a tiny middle and six evenly distributed extremities—a long, thin head, a tail, two arms, and two legs. As he rotated, three members were always touching the ground and three were in the air; those on the ground were always legs and tail, and those in the air were always head and arms.

When the Queen had draped his award over his head, he rolled over to face the audience, with the result that the ribbon hung from his tail. He then sang the following song, to my surprise and great pleasure, for I had written it once and put it in a book:

The Mrs. kr. Mr.
Then how her Mr. kr.!
He kr. kr. kr.
Until he raised a blr.
The blr. killed his Mrs.;
Then how he mr. krs.!
He mr. mr. mr.
Until he kr. sr.
He covered her with krs.
Till she became his Mrs.
The Mrs. kr. Mr.
(And so on and on and on . . .)

**Abbreviatio**   a BRAYV ee ah tee oh   (L. "shortening").
A shortened form of a word or phrase used chiefly in writing to represent the complete form.

Many words are commonly written as abbreviations. We write *Mass.* (or, in the postal zip code, *MA*) for *Massachusetts; A.M.* for *Ante Meridiem; P.M.* for *Post Meridiem* (or *post mortem*).

Abbreviatio reasoned that since the abbreviation of *Mister* is *Mr.*, it follows that the abbreviation of *kissed her* should be *kr.;* of *blister, blr.;* of *missed her, mr.;* and of *sister, sr.* And since the abbreviation of *Missus* (earlier *Mistress*) is *Mrs.*, obviously the abbreviation of *kisses* must be *krs.* By the same logic, one might drop all vowels from the printed language, reducing the final paragraph of a recent *Wall Street Journal* editorial to this:

Mr. Rgn sms t ndrstnd ths dspt lvng wthn sght f th Wshngtn mnmnt. t s fr frm clr tht hs cnmc prgrm hs fld, nd vn lss clr tht tx bsts wld b th prpr rmd f t ds. T thrw n th twl n ths rl rnd wld b cptltn nt mrl n th Rgn dmnstrtn's cnmc thrs bt n th vw f gvrnmnt t ws lctd t prs.

(Which, in case you did not follow, reads, in the clear:)

Mr. Reagan seems to understand this despite living within sight of the Washington monument. It is far from clear that his economic program has failed, and even less clear that tax boosts would be the proper remedy if it does. To throw in the towel in this early round would be a capitulation not merely on the Reagan administration's economic theories but on the view of government it was elected to pursue.

**F**ROM up the hill came a loud voice: "Equal time! Equal time!" I saw a yellow mongrel dog coming down; he had a black patch over his right eye, a begging cup in his left paw, and a whiskey bottle in his right; he wavered from side to side, and after each call for equal time he tipped the bottle to his mouth.

"That's ACYROLOGIA!" screamed the Gardener, leveling a tong in the dog's direction, and jumping up and down on his poker leg in rage. "Seize him! Throw him out!" Immediately a boa constrictor wearing spectacles glided from the crowd and coiled tightly about the dog's body, pinning him fast; but he continued to shout, "Equal time! Equal time!"

"Nay, friend Gardener," said the Queen in a sweet voice that yet carried all the way up the hill. "Though Acyrologia is to receive no honors from us, let him be heard. Speech is free in the Garden." At this the serpent uncoiled itself and slid away into the crowd. Acyrologia leered about him, bobbed his head, and resumed his progress to the platform, staggering now, and changing his shout to: "Free speech! Free speech!"

"Who is that?" I asked the red imp.

"He was once the Queen's chief minister, as the Gardener is now," said the imp. "But he plotted with the Solecisms, and nearly lost us our Garden. The Queen recruited the Gardener then, because he could blow so hard. We should have slain that yellow dog, but she was too soft-hearted. She gave him his freedom, and he has been wandering about the Garden ever since, begging for coins and whiskey and scraps."

Acyrologia lurched to the stage; ignoring the Queen, he turned to the audience and burst into this roundel, the words of which led me to suspect that he did not see himself as others saw him:

> Don't tell *me* no grammatic rules:
>     Hey, man, I get on good enough.
>     I don't talk like no powder puff,
> But ladies looks at me and drools,
> And feels my chest in swimming pools—
>     Talk ain't no match for he-man stuff.
> Don't tell *me* no grammatic rules;
>     Hey, man, I get on good enough.

> Man, when did junk you learns in schools
>     Help anyone when times gets tough?
>     I thumbs my nose; I calls your bluff.
> I leaves that sissy stuff to fools.
> Don't tell *me* no grammatic rules.

As he completed his song, he was seized by a quartet of bulldogs wearing bobby helmets and carrying truncheons. They hustled him up the hill and flung him summarily out the gate, while he continued to shout: "Free speech! Equal time!"

**Acyrologia**   a see roh LOHJ ee uh   (Gr. "improperly used word or saying").
The incorrect use of language.

Any abuse of language is acyrology. It comprises every sort of grammatical error, including the use of adjectives for adverbs and adverbs for adjectives; of single subjects with plural verbs and plural subjects with singular verbs; of words for others of unlike meaning. It includes also disagreement between pronoun and antecedent, lack of subordination, clumsy subordination, incoherence, incomplete comparisons, missing connections, dangling modifiers, mixed metaphors, illogical sentence structure, double negatives, omission of essential words, phrases misused as sentences, ambiguities, and irrelevancies.

A few of the misdeeds of acyrology:

He drove most of the way at ninety miles an hour, flaunting the law. (To flaunt is to show off; to flout is to show contempt for. He was *flouting* the law.)

He inferred in his speech that I was a crook. (To infer is to deduce. He hinted —that is, *implied*—that I was a crook.)

Of the two warm days, Sunday was warmest. (When only two things are compared, the adjective takes the comparative, not the superlative. Sunday was *warmer.*)

The screeching of seagulls fill the air. (The subject of the sentence is "screeching," not "seagulls." The screeching of seagulls *fills* the air.)

**Vicious circle**

The poet George Barker, in his short novel *The Dead Seagull,* has the following real or pretended quotation: "They cut down elms to build asylums for people driven mad by the cutting down of elms."

—*Word Ways*

A LLITERATIO was a cockatoo of many colors. She stuttered down the hill, stop and go, uttering a different consonant with each hop. "K-k-k-k-k!" she cried; and then: "T-t-t-t!" and then: "S-s-s-s-s!" She approached the Queen saying: "M-m-m-m-m!" and accepted her award saying: "L-l-l-l-l!" Afterward she sang:

"Alliteration's artful aid"—
That is what the poet said:
"Sing a song of silliness";
"King and queen and court caress";
"Babes blow bubbles in a box";
"Saints may sing when sewing socks";
"Down the drain the donkeys dive";
"Lions leave the lambs alive."
(See? You needn't be a great
Genius to alliterate.)

**Alliteratio**   a lit uh RAHT ee oh   (L. "letter-tagging").
A repetition of the same beginning sound in each of a series of words.

The nattering nabobs of negativism. —Spiro Agnew
The fair breeze blew, the white foam flew, / The furrow followed free.
   —Coleridge, "The Rime of the Ancient Mariner"
Last but not least.
Cool, calm, and collected.
Footloose and fancy-free.
Peter Piper picked a peck of pickled peppers.

---

### Schizophrenic words

*Best* and *worst* both mean "to defeat." *Cleave* means both "to cling to" and "to split apart." *Fast* means both "speedy" and "immobilized" (as well as several other things). *Dress* means to put on apparel, as a person does, or to take it off, as is done to a chicken. And while you are reflecting on such oddities, you may as well know that *bleach* means also "blacking"; *bluefish* also "greenfish"; *bosom* also "depression"; *emancipate* also "to enslave"; and *help* also "to hinder."

## Double meaning

The use of an ungrammatical word or phrase that creates an *ambiguity* (page 47). Double meanings are not to be confused with double entendres (but are kissing kin to Irish bulls).

> At breakfast this morning the mess line didn't move fast enough to suit one of the KPs who slap out the food. To expedite things, he told the GIs as they passed him, "Let's keep one feet moving, men. Keep one feet moving." —*Yank* (From the collection of linguist Allen Walker Read)

The late Frank Sullivan believed there are persons who have a special gift for double meanings, which he called wolf sentences in sheep's clothing. A particularly brilliant exemplar of the form, he said, was one Dave Clark of Broadway. Once during an argument Mr. Clark exclaimed: "Well, I may be wrong, but I'm not far from it!" Asked for his opinion of a new play, he replied, "Oh, don't miss it if you can!"

A certain lady of Hollywood, said Sullivan, uttered these "wolf sentences":

> There are lots of nice people in Hollywood—but not many.
> This is the best salad I ever put in my whole mouth.
> Oh, it was a heck of a party—everybody in the room was there.
> A whole bunch of men came in surrounded by a little fellow in the middle.
> She had more money than she could afford.
> Two can live as cheaply as one, but it costs twice as much.

(My mother occasionally purveyed double meanings. "Oh," she told a visitor, "I haven't been to South Bend since the last time I was there.")

T HE next to be honored was AMBIGUITY, a ship's compass sprouting arms and legs; in his wake came four smaller compasses, identified by stickers on their faces as AMPHIBOLOGIA, NOEMA, INNUENDO, and DOUBLE ENTENDRE. Ambiguity, Amphibologia, and Noema nodded at members of the audience as they went by; Innuendo and Double Entendre did not nod, but winked. The compass needles, instead of pointing north, spun at random around their dials. Pity the poor mariner who relied on one of those for a bearing!

The Queen decorated Ambiguity, after which the five compasses sang as follows:

*Ambiguity:*
I'm Ambiguity, a trope
That walks the earth in shapes galore.

*Amphibologia:*
As: Fear you, sweet, that I'm no more
In love? —No, *more* in love, dear dope!

*Noema:*
As: Noon on two, and dawn on four,
And eve on three I trudge life's slope.*

*Innuendo:*
As: I have read you. Dare I hope
You know words need an editor?

*Double Entendre:*
As: England's wolves have ceased to cope;
The fairies shooed them out the door.†

*In chorus:*
We speak with sense ulterior.
Don't be ashamed if you're agrope—
    We walk the earth in shapes galore.

**Ambiguity**   am buh GY$\overline{OO}$ i tee   (L. "wandering about").
Obscurity of expression.

*The Sphinx's riddle, answered by Oedipus: "Man, who walks on four as a babe, on two as a man, and in old age on three, using a cane."
†Poet Rose Fyleman's innocent double entendre was:

> There are no wolves in England any more;
> The fairies have driven them all away.

Ambiguity is the presence of two or more possible meanings in any passage, usually because of faulty expression. An ambiguity resulting from a slip in grammar is *amphibologia* (Gr. "ambiguous speech"). A deliberate ambiguity is *noema* (Gr. "idea"). An ambiguity with a depreciatory hint or suggestion is *innuendo* (L. "giving a nod, insinuating"). An ambiguity in which one of the possible meanings is risqué is *double entendre* (Fr. "ambiguity").

*Ambiguity:* She told her mother she was getting fat. (There is no way to know whether the second *she* refers to the daughter or the mother.)

## Amphibologia  (am fi boh LOHJ ee uh)

John was absent at the first practice game, which caused much comment. (*Which* has no antecedent unless it refers to the first practice game, which seems unlikely.) My husband is a ballet dancer, but I don't know anything about it. (*It* has no antecedent.)

Or the meaning may change with a change in punctuation:

| | |
|---|---|
| Private. No swimming allowed. | Private: No. Swimming allowed. |
| The butler stood by the door and called the guests' names as they arrived. | The butler stood by the door and called the guests names as they arrived. |
| I'm sorry you can't come with us. | I'm sorry. You can't come with us. |

Lawrence Casler reports in *Verbatim* that a dinner speaker asked the master of ceremonies to introduce him as follows:

> Ladies and gentlemen, I bring you a man among men. He is out of place when among cheaters and scoundrels. He feels quite at home when surrounded by persons of integrity. He is uncomfortable when not helping others. He is perfectly satisfied when his fellow human beings are happy. He tries to make changes in order for the country to be a better place. He should leave us this evening with feelings of disgust at ineptitude and a desire to do better. I present to you Mr. John Smith.

But somehow the master of ceremonies, or perhaps his secretary, mispunctuated the passage, and it came out this way:

> Ladies and gentlemen, I bring you a man. Among men, he is out of place. When among cheaters and scoundrels, he feels quite at home. When surrounded by persons of integrity, he is uncomfortable. When not helping others, he is perfectly satisfied. When his fellow human beings are happy, he tries to make changes. In order for the country to be a better place, he should leave us this evening. With feelings of disgust at ineptitude and a desire to do better, I present to you Mr. John Smith.

**Noema** (noh EEM uh)   may be either an enigma or utter nonsense, as is this passage by the eighteenth-century British writer Samuel Foote:

> So she went into the garden to cut a cabbage-leaf to make an apple pie, and at the same time, a great she-bear coming up the street pops its head into the shop. What! No soap! So he died; and she very imprudently married the barber; and there were present the Picninnies, and the Joblillies, and the Garyulies, and the Grand Panjandrum himself, with the little round button on top. And they all fell to playing the game of catch as catch can, till the gunpowder ran out of the heels of their boots.

When the king asked Hamlet how he fared, he was answered in a Noema:

> Excellent, i' faith; of the chameleon's dish; I eat the air, promise crammed; you cannot feed capons so.

**Innuendo** (in yōō END oh)   implies more than it says:

> She seems a nice girl, but I don't understand what keeps her out so late at night.
> No doubt George is honest, but I wouldn't leave my pocketbook lying around.

> There was a young lady named Etta
> Who fancied herself in a sweater.
> > Three reasons she had:
> > To keep warm was not bad,
> But the other two reasons were better. —Unknown

A **double entendre** (DUHB ool ahn TAHN druh)   is frequently off color in its second interpretation, as is Charles Dickens's description (in *Martin Chuzzlewit*) of an elderly church organist's infatuation with a member of the choir:

> She touched his organ and from that bright epoch, even it, the old companion of his happiest hours, incapable as he had thought of elevation, began a new and deified existence.

**A**NADIPLOSIS was a caterpillar as long as a man is high, and thick proportionately; it was perhaps of the inchworm family, since it made its way to the platform by arching its body in the air until the tail end met the front, then stretching forward and repeating the process. After receiving its medal, Anadiplosis sang several songs, to much applause, but the only one I remember is this:

> How dangerous it is to *think!*—
>  To think too much may lead to *know;*
> To know too much may lead to *drink;*
>  To drink too much may lead to *throw*
> *All thought of thinking down the sink.*
> How dangerous it is to think!

## Anadiplosis   an uh dī PLOHS is   (Gr. "doubling back").

Word repetition. Specifically, the repetition of a word that ends one clause at the beginning of the next.

Peacham says that anadiplosis "doth as it were strike a double note, or rehearse the last word again":

> All service ranks the same with God, / With God, whose puppets, best and worst, / Are we. —Robert Browning, *Pippa Passes*
> With death, death must be recompensed; on mischief, mischief must be heaped. —Ovid
> Never trouble trouble till trouble troubles you. —Benjamin Franklin
> Men in great place are thrice servants: servants of the sovereign or state; servants of fame; and servants of business. —Francis Bacon

The following example of anadiplosis is a sonnet in which the first sound of each succeeding line echoes the last sound of the previous line. It is borrowed from one of my earlier books:

> I scarce recall when first you said hello.
> "Hello!" said I, too young to realize
> Lies were your *vade mecum.* (Spiders so
> Sew webs, and lie in wait for hapless flies.)
> Flies time so fast? Why is it I can know
> No more that lying lovelight in your eyes?
> I scarce recall—it was so long ago—
> A golden time, before I grew too wise.
>
> Why's wisdom executioner of youth?
> You thought I left because you lied. Not I!
> I left when you began to tell the truth:
> Truth comes too dear for coinless youth to buy.
> By lies I might regain you, after all.
> Although—so long ago—I scarce recall.

Variants of anadiplosis have their own names. Here are some:

## Anaphora   a NAF uh ruh   (Gr. "repetition").
The repetition of a word or phrase at the beginning of several successive clauses, paragraphs, or verses:

> We shall not flag or fail. We shall go on to the end. We shall fight in France, we shall fight on the seas and oceans, we shall fight with growing confidence and growing strength in the air, we shall defend our island, whatever the cost may be, we shall fight on the beaches, . . . we shall fight in the fields and in the streets, . . . we shall never surrender. —Winston Churchill

## Antimetabole   an ti me TAB oh lee   (Gr. "in the opposite direction; turning about").
The repetition of two words next to each other, but in reverse order:

> The rooster said, "Pray be my hen" (he said, said he);
> "I'll not, and pray don't ask again" (she said, said she).

## Epanalepsis   e pa nuh LEP sis   (Gr. "taking again").
The repetition of the first word of a line at the end of the same line:

> Common sense is not so common. —Voltaire

## Onomastikos   on oh MAS ti kohs   (Gr. "naming").
The study of the origin of names.

Amelia is a name of Teutonic origin meaning "industrious." But before naming your next daughter Amelia, you might consider that in the branch of medicine devoted to the study of monstrosities, the name designates absence of limbs. And it would be advisable not to call your next son Amelius, for the same reason.

NASTROPHE's stomach was his head; his arms emerged from his ears; his legs stood not side by side, but one behind the other. His thanks to the Queen took the form of a triolet:

> You my again have suit refused;
>> Wooed you have I; me you have slain.
> Adored you I; me you misused.
> You my again have suit refused;
> Joked not when I were you amused.
>> Me have with treated you disdain.
> You my again have suit refused;
>> Wooed you have I; me you have slain.

**Anastrophe**   a NAS troh fee   (Gr. "turning upside down; turning back").

The inversion of the normal order of words, as in "Up the hill went Jack and Jill."

> No war or battle's sound / Was heard the world around.
> Me he restored, and him he hanged.
> Backward run the sentences until reels the mind. —Wolcott Gibbs on the style of *Time* magazine
> In the bosom of her respectable family resided Camilla. —Fanny Burney

Charles M. Doughty, a writer of the early twentieth century whose interest lay more in style than in substance, made life difficult for his readers by regularly inverting his words. These examples are from his *Travels in Arabia Deserta*:

> Two chiefly are the perils in Arabia: famine and the dreadful-faced harpy of their religion. . . . Clear was the weather. . . . Sorry were his benefactors, that he whom they lately dismissed alive lay now a dead carcass in the wilderness; themselves might so mishap another day in the great deserts. . . . Pleasant is the summer evening air of this high wilderness. . . . In whatever house he entered at supper time, he might sit down with the rest to eat and welcome, but they grudged that he should carry any morsel away. . . . Pleasant was the sight of their tilled ground.

An intentional deviation from usual word order, not necessarily a reversal, is a *hyperbaton*   hī PUR buh ton   (Gr. "stepping over"):

> Yet I'll not shed her blood,
> Nor scar that whiter skin of hers than snow.
>> —Shakespeare, *Othello*

FROM her appearance, ANTAPODOSIS was either a grandfather's clock in the voluptuous shape of a Gibson girl, or a Gibson girl who looked like a clock. I was not sure which, even after she had received her award and sung this song:

Antapodosis—like a woman I,
And since a woman, also like a clock:
My hands and face are pretty to espy,
My movement is an easy tick and tock;
And when I'm out of order, and my gait
Runs fast or slow, I'm hard to regulate.

**Antapodosis**  an ta PAHD oh sis  (Gr. "giving back; requital").
An extended simile.

Conversation is but carving!
Give no more to every guest
Than he's able to digest.
Give him always of the prime,
And but little at a time.
Carve to all but just enough,
And that you may have your due,
Let your neighbor carve for you.
—Jonathan Swift, "Conversation"

Energy in a nation is like sap in a tree; it rises from the bottom up; it does not come from the top down. When I was a schoolmaster, I used to say that the trouble about the college sophomore was that the sap of manhood was rising in him, but hadn't reached his head. —Woodrow Wilson

**Polypteton**  poh LIP tuh tahn  (Gr. "many purposes").
The repetition of the same word or root with different grammatical functions or forms.

Few men speak humbly of humility, chastely of chastity, skeptically of skepticism. —Pascal
Let the people think they govern, and they will be governed.
—William Penn

NTIPHRASIS was called, and got shakily to his feet, or rather his hind hooves, supporting himself on a hawthorn stick. He seemed to be facing us and facing away from us at the same time; I could see all of him at once. "I'm too old," he bleated, "too old, too old. My young friend Ironia will take my award with his when his turn comes."

"We understand," said the Queen. "But would you not at least sing us a song, dear Antiphrasis?"

"I will try, I will try," he quavered; and this is what he sang:

Although he called me very wise, I knew he meant a dolt;
He said, "Dear sir, you're much too kind"—I knew that *kind* meant *mean;*
I knew he meant a swaybacked mare when calling it a colt;
He called me "so experienced," and meant "so grassy green."
It's always that way with some folks—though honesty they prize,
They find it easier to make their points contrariwise.

**Antiphrasis**   an TIF ruh sis   (Gr. "expressing by the opposite").
The use of a word in a sense opposite to the proper meaning.

In antiphrasis, "How wise you are!" is likely to mean: "What a fool you are!" If the reader or listener takes the phrase literally, of course, the trick doesn't work.

> Brothers and sisters, friends and enemies, I just can't believe everyone in here is a friend and I don't want to leave anyone out. —Malcolm X

Antiphrasis may overlap *sarcasmus* (page 130):

> Oh, what a hard time you are having, to be sure! (That is, "Come now—you aren't so badly off.")
> Well, here's a pretty state of things! (Meaning, "Well, here's a real mess!")

And it may overlap *actio* (page 38), since what is said is less revealing than the way of saying it.

T HE next helper to be honored was ANTITHESIS, who was at once male and female, tall and short, plump and meager. I no sooner thought her coloring dull than his turned radiant, nor his voice shrill than hers was sweet. After receiving the Queen's decoration, he, she, or it sang this villanelle:

"I sing of prose, and poetry;
Of facts I sing, and fiction too,"
Antithesis explained to me—

"Of good and evil; huge and wee;
Divorce and marriage; me and you—
I sing of prose and poetry.

Of dissonance and harmony
I sing; of Gentile and of Jew,"
Antithesis explained to me.

"I sing of pride and modesty;
Of cowardice and derring-do;
I sing of prose, and poetry.

Of what has been, and what will be,
I sing; of what is old and new,"
Antithesis explained to me.

"My song is of the slave and free,
The parting, and the rendezvous.
I sing of prose, and poetry,"
Antithesis explained to me.

**Antithesis**   an TITH uh sis   (Gr. "opposition").
The juxtaposition of contrasting ideas in balanced phrases.

Opposites increase each other—black and white, low and high, happy and sad. Often not just words but whole sentences are coupled together by contraries. "Contrariety of two words thus," says Peacham: "I have loved peace, and not loathed it; I have saved his life, and not destroyed it. Contrariety of sentences thus: among the wicked, simplicity is counted foolishness, and craftiness high wisdom; flattery is friendship, and faithfulness made fraud; sin is succored, and righteousness rent in sunder."

Measures, not men.
The prodigal robs his heir; the miser robs himself.
Crafty men condemn studies; simple men admire them; and wise men use them.
He for God only, she for God in him. —Milton, *Paradise Lost*

As love, if love be perfect, casts out fear, / So hate, if hate be perfect, casts out fear. —Tennyson, *Merlin and Vivien*

Detestation of the high is the involuntary homage of the low. —Dickens, *A Tale of Two Cities*

Naked came I out of my mother's womb, and naked shall I return thither. —Job I, 21

Love is an ideal thing, marriage a real thing. —Goethe

Forty years of romance make a woman look like a ruin and forty years of marriage make her look like a public building. —Oscar Wilde

From a scientific point of view, this was an exciting step forward. Emotionally, it was shipwreck. —Peter Dickinson, *The Poison Oracle*

Ring out the darkness of the land, / Ring in the Christ that is to be. —Tennyson, *In Memoriam*

Alexander Pope on Lord Harvey, whom he called "himself one vile antithesis":

> Amphibious thing! that acting either part,
> The trifling head, or the corrupted heart,
> Fop at the toilet, flatterer at the board,
> Now trips a lady, and now struts a lord . . .
> Beauty that shocks you, parts that none will trust,
> Wit that can creep, and pride that licks the dust.

**Autolog**   AWT oh lahg   (Gr. "same word").
A self-descriptive word.

> In this sentence, the word *and* occurs twice, the word *eight* occurs twice, the word *four* occurs twice, the word *fourteen* occurs four times, the word *in* occurs twice, the word *occurs* occurs fourteen times, the word *sentence* occurs twice, the word *the* occurs fourteen times, the word *this* occurs twice, the word *times* occurs seven times, the word *twice* occurs eight times, the word *seven* occurs twice, and the word *word* occurs fourteen times. —Howard Bergerson, in *Word Ways*

T HE Gardener called ANTONOMASIA and PROSONOMASIA. They descended hand in hand, two boys not yet at puberty, as angelic of face as choirboys. One wore a silvery shirt and golden trousers, and the other a shirt that seemed silver and trousers that seemed gold; these so winked and glittered that they held my eyes fast. If I had had the naming of them, I thought, I would have called them not as the Gardener did, but something more fitting—Goldy and Silvy, or the like. They danced prettily for us after the ceremony of awarding, and sang each a little song:

> *Antonomasia:*
> Since Casanova's dallyings
>> Brought many maids *ad ova,*
> We tut at men who do such things,
>> And call them Casanova.

> *Prosonomasia:*
> John Gerald Jones's great delight
>> Was carving folks to kipper;
> Folks do not call him Johnny Jones—
>> They call him Jack the Ripper.

**Antonomasia**   an toh noh MAYZ ee uh   (Gr. "naming instead"). The substitution of a title or an epithet for a proper name, or of a personal name for a common name to designate a member of a group or class.

**Prosonomasia**   proh soh noh MAYZ ee uh   (Gr. "naming"). Nicknaming, frequently by means of a pun.

Antonomasia says "Your Majesty" to a king, "Your Lordship" to a nobleman, "Your Excellency" to an ambassador, substituting the name of an office, profession, study, art, or dignity for a proper name. It may turn a name into a common noun: Quisling into *quisling* because of Vidkun Quisling's treason in World War II; Apollo into *apollo* because of the god's handsomeness; Babbitt into *babbitt* because of George F. Babbitt's narrow-minded conformity; Solomon into *solomon* on account of his wisdom.

Prosonomasia defines a person or thing by some characteristic: the Conqueror (William I of England); the dismal science (political economy); the king of beasts (the lion); the Father of Lies (Satan): the great unwashed (the populace); the Iron Duke (Wellington); the Jolly Roger (pirate flag); the Knight of the Rueful Countenance (Don Quixote); and so on.*

You can probably identify the following present and past personalities from their nicknames:

The Wizard of Menlo Park · The Manassa Mauler · The "It" Girl · The Brown Bomber · The Great Commoner · The Little Flower · The Prisoner of Chillon · The Rail-Splitter

(In case you missed any, the persons named are: Thomas A. Edison; Jack Dempsey; Clara Bow; Joe Louis; William Jennings Bryan; Fiorello La Guardia; François de Bonnivard; Abraham Lincoln.)

*For a list of more than a hundred such sobriquets, see Fowler's *Modern English Usage*.

T HEN summoned were APHAERESIS, SYNCOPE, and APOCOPE; but only one creature responded. It had the head and wings of an eagle and the body and hindquarters of a lion; its tail was a writhing serpent with a hissing head of its own at the tip. The union of the three parts was provisional, for when the Queen hung a purple ribbon around its neck, saying, "In your honor, Aphaeresis," the head and wings separated from the rest and hung before her in the air, an eagle-headed cherub. No sign remained on the body of where the joining had been; it stood there placidly while she arranged another ribbon around its midsection, and scratched its back, saying, "Syncope." The tail then dropped away, coiled, and lifted its serpent snout so that she could hang the last ribbon, saying "Apocope." Afterward the three parts reunited as casually as they had split, and the eagle head sang as follows, while the serpent hissed in the background:

> To Aph-a-er-e-sis Lord Language said,
>> "Words grow too proud; they stand disgusting tall.
> Aph, bring one down to size—chop off its head!
>> Impale that member on my castle wall!"
>
> *Especial* was the word Aph chose to fall;
>> He lopped the *E*. But though poor *special* bled,
> It flourished still, a little bit more small.
>> Then Syn-co-pe was ordered blood to shed:
>
> "Syn, gut thou words too fat and overfed;
>> From *idololatry* strike middle -*ol*-:
> *Idolatry! Pacificist* instead
>> Shrink down to *pacifist!* Cut fat with tall!"
>
> A-poc-o-pe was next to hear his call:
>> "Ap, *mine* and *singen* both have tails to shed.
> Turn *mine* to *my;* for *singen, sing* install.
>> Cut tail away as well as guts and head!"
>
> (Now, Aph-a-er-e-sis did murder dread,
>> And ripping guts did Syn-co-pe appal;
> A-poc-o-pe shed tears for tails that bled;
>> Yet on command they sent words to the wall.)
>
> I cried, "Lord, I for mercy to thee crawl;
>> Pray, doom no more these words—words thou hast bred!
> Extend thy mercy to them, and withal
>> To Syn-co-pe, A-poc-o-pe," I pled,
> ". . . And Aph-a-er-e-sis!"

**Aphaeresis**    a fi AYR uh sis    (Gr. "taking away").
The loss of an initial letter or syllable in a word.

As the generations pass, pronunciation, and after it (but haltingly) spelling, evolve up paths laid out in the philological laws uncovered by such linguistic scholars as Jacob Grimm. *P* over the centuries, for instance, changed ineluctably into *f,* and *t* into *th,* turning *pater* into *father.*

Some of these changes involve the shortening of words. When the first syllable or sound of a word falls away, the process is called *aphaeresis.* Thus, the *adder* was once a *nadder. Cute,* defined as "delightfully pretty or dainty," was once *acute,* which survives in the sense of "shrewd."

An elision within a word is a **syncope**   SIN koh pee    (Gr. "cutting together"). *Never* becomes *ne'er; launderess, laundress; jewellery, jewelry; mistress, missus.*

> Thou thy worldly task hast done, / Home art gone, and ta'en thy wages.
> —Shakespeare, *Cymbeline.*

The loss of a final sound in a word is **apocope**   a PAHK oh pee. Anglo-Saxon *singen* became our *sing; ie* became *I.*

> I am Sir Oracle, and when / I ope my mouth let no dog bark. —Shakespeare, *A Midsummer Night's Dream*

> You see this pebble-stone? It's a thing I bought
> Of a bit of a chit of a boy i' the mid o' day.
> I like to dock the smaller parts-o'-speech,
> As we curtail the already cur-tail'd cur.
> —C. S. Calverley

A current example of apocope is the tendency to drop the final *g* sound in words ending in an unaccented *-ing*—*goin', sayin', tellin', lovin':*

> Noah an' Jonah an' Cap'n John Smith,
> Mariners, travelers, magazines of myth,
> Settin' up in heaven, chewin' and a-chawin',
> Eatin' their tebaccy, talkin' and a-jawin'.
> —Don Marquis, *Noah an' Jonah an' Cap'n John Smith*

The omission of a vowel, often when two words are combined into one, is **synaloepha**   sin uh LEEF ah    (Gr. "melting together"). Examples are: *it's, isn't, shan't, can't;* in poetry: *th'angels* for *the angels.*

### Venereal noun

A noun denoting a collection of persons or things regarded as a unit, defining them through word play.

The notion of desire and pursuit being common to love and the hunt, and Venus being goddess of both, sportsmen of the Middle Ages applied the term "venereal" to collective nouns naming the animals they hunted. The term now includes any collective noun built on a trick of language. In *An Exaltation of Larks* (Grossman Publishers, 1968) James Lipton lists six families of venereal nouns, as follows:

1. Onomatopoeia (a murmuration of starlings; a gaggle of geese).
2. Characteristic (a leap of leopards; a skulk of foxes).
3. Appearance (a knot of toads; a bouquet of pheasants).
4. Habitat (a shoal of bass; a nest of rabbits).
5. Comment, pro or con, reflecting the observer's point of view (a richness of martens; a cowardice of curs).
6. Error, resulting from an incorrect transcription that has been preserved in the language (a school—originally *shoal*—of fish).

The creation of venereal nouns has become a popular pastime since Mr. Lipton's book appeared. These are from Mary Ann Madden's competition page in *New York* magazine:

A riot of students · A peck of kisses · A mine of egotists · A host of parasites · A complement of sycophants · A range of ovens · A furrow of brows · A nun of your business · A lot of realtors · A knot of Windsors · A wagon of teetotalers

*Word Ways* offers these venereal terms for collections of prostitutes:

A flourish of strumpets · An essay of trollops · A herd of harlots · A pride of loins · An anthology of pros · A jam of tarts · A peal of Jezebels · A troop of whores · A smelting of whores · An expanse of broads · A chapter of trollops · A fanfare of strumpets

**A**POPHASIS was next named. He was a red fox, with a proud brush of a tail; his eyes, too, were red, and shifty. "I am unworthy of this honor," he cried out as he came down the hill. "I cannot accept it!" But when the Queen said, "Very well, then," he hastened his pace, and took his medal with alacrity before singing this triolet, winking at us first one red eye and then the other:

> Not mine to dwell on your besottedness;
> > Not mine to mention that you cheat at games.
> Your love of lying is not mine to stress.
> Not mine to dwell on your besottedness,
> > Or bruit abroad your infamy with dames.
> Not mine to dwell on your besottedness;
> > Not mine to mention that you cheat at games.

**Apophasis**   a PAHF uh sis   (Gr. "denial").
The mention of something in disclaiming intention of mentioning it.

A political opponent of Senator Edward Kennedy told an audience: "Let us make no judgment on the events at Chappaquiddick, since the facts are not yet all in." His listeners knew, though, that he was making a judgment, and asking them to concur in it. The same twist of rhetoric can be used to brag without seeming to: "I have no need to list all I have done for you; the record speaks for itself."

Kissin' kin to apophasis is:

**Paralepsis**   pa ra LEP sis   (Gr. "disregard").
Emphasis of a point by seeming to pass over it: "I confine to this page the volume of his treacheries and debaucheries."

> In view of this painful possibility [that I am charged with writing nonsense] I will not (as I might) appeal indignantly to my other writings as a proof that I am incapable of such a deed: I will not (as I might) point to the strong moral purpose of this poem itself, to the arithmetical principles so cautiously inculcated in it, or to its noble teachings in Natural History. —Lewis Carroll, Preface to "The Hunting of the Snark"

**T**HE Gardener called "Aporia," and a donkey came by on his hind legs, mincing. When the Queen had graced his neck with the ribbon, he turned toward the audience, brayed loudly, and sang as follows:

> There was an ass who starved to death, they say,
> From indecision 'twixt two heaps of hay.
> Not I, Aporia: though I may feign
> Uncertainty between two piles of grain,
> It's but to stress the plenty in my stall—
> I end by bending neck, and munching all.

## Aporia   a POR ee uh   (Gr. "without passage").

Real or affected perplexity as to what to say from all that might be said.

Unlike apophasis and paralepsis, aporia, rather than disclaiming intention of describing an adversary's faults, complains how hard it is to choose among such abundance.

> She was wanton, she was lascivious, she was faithless, and, worse, she was unkind: of what shall I first complain? —Peacham

Aporia may also be a claimed perplexity as to what to say in praise, or indeed in any description at all.

> A virginal air, large blue eyes very soulful and appealing, a dazzling fair skin, a supple and resilient body, a touching voice, teeth of ivory and the loveliest blond hair, there you have a sketch of this charming creature whose naive graces and delicate traits are beyond our power to describe. —De Sade

## Anaphora   a NAF uh ruh   (Gr. "bringing back").

Marked repetition of a word or phrase in successive clauses or sentences.

> At her feet he bowed, he fell, he lay down; at her feet he bowed, he fell; where he bowed, there he fell down dead.
> There is no mistake; there has been no mistake; and there shall be no mistake. —Duke of Wellington

T HERE took shape on the stage a magnified bird's nest, knitted of branches instead of straws and twigs. The Gardener called, "APOSIOPESIS," and a roc, of the sort that carry off elephants as food for their young, dropped from the sky, not diving, as I would have expected, but darting like a monstrous swallow. For a moment she fluttered over the nest, as if wondering whether to settle there; then fluttered toward the Queen, then back again, continuing this pantomime of two-mindedness until the Gardener, crying, "Enough already," seized a yellow claw, and pulled her down to the platform. After receiving her decoration, she darted again to the nest, but still could not make up her mind to stop there. The Gardener snapped, "My dear woman, the eggs are your own; for goodness' sake, start brooding. It's your job to hatch them."

"If only I could be sure it is the right thing to do!" said the roc in a worried tone; and as she settled on the nest she proceeded to sing this rondeau:

> "If you would only, dear . . . " begged he.
> "It's just that . . . never mind," said she.
> "I wish you'd . . . what I mean . . . " he sighed.
> "You really wish I'd . . .?" she replied.
> "Of course I do . . . that is . . you see . . . "
> "I do feel sort of . . . " "Same for me . . ."
> "It makes me so . . ." "Me too . . . if we . . ."
> "Do you suppose . . . ?" "If you had tried . . ."
>     "If you would only . . ."
>
> "If anyone knew . . ." "Fiddle-dee . . .
> They wouldn't . . ." "You can't guarantee . . ."
> "I'm losing patience. Let's decide.
> I'm asking you to be my bride . . .
> For better . . . worse . . . eternity.
>     If you would only . . ."

**Aposiopesis**   a pah sī oh PEES is   (Gr. "maintaining silence").
An unfinished thought.

In aposiopesis, the speaker leads up to a key word until his listeners have it clearly in mind, but then stops: "as," says Peacham, "thou naughty, vile, and errant . . . keeping villain or thief in the mouth still, for fear lest the other should take advantage of a slander." Aposiopesis is a variant of *ellipsis*, at which you will arrive in due course.

I might say much more, but modesty demands silence.
If we should fail—!
Oh, go to—!
Well, I never!
" 'Well, if you *will* wear *décolleté*,' said the princess loftily, and went off to look
for water and towel." —Walter

AUXESIS came on stage—a hippopotamus, save that she walked on not four but eight stumpy legs, which moved ponderously, and so slowly that she might have been a funeral procession all by herself. Having accepted her medal, she sang along the following lines:

> Auxesis' tread deliberate I hear,
>     Step piled on step. So word is piled on word:
> "The seed; the ear; the corn upon the ear . . ."
>     "An egg; and thence a chick; and thence a bird—
> That bird an eagle . . ." Or: "Without a nail,
>     The shoe was lost; without a shoe, the horse . . ."
> And so on. Or: "First smile; then grin; then gale
>     Of laughter." Word on word, with rising force.
> Thus Pope on vice: "Familiar with her face,
> We first endure, then pity, then embrace."

**Auxesis**   awk SEES is   (Gr. "amplification").
1. The use of a more high-flown word for one that is proper. 2. A gradual increase in intensity of meaning.

In its first meaning, auxesis is an embellishment which, says Smith's *Rhetorick,* substitutes for the applicable word "one that is more grave and magnificent," containing elements of both exaggeration and hyperbole. Peacham states that by auxesis, "the orator doth make a low dwarf a tall fellow; of pebble stones, pearls; and of thistles, mighty oaks." He continues: "As to say one is slain, when he is but a little beaten; to call him an arrant thief, that once stole a trifle. Contrariwise, to call an honest man, a saint; an honest woman, a holy matron; a fair maiden, an angel."

In its second meaning, auxesis advances step by step toward a climax:

John found the food indifferent; Dick considered it abhorrent; Harry killed the cook.

He lost besides his children and his wife, / His realms, renown, liege, liberty and life. —George Puttenham, *English Poesie* (1589)

. . . enflamed with the study of learning and the admiration of virtue; stirred up with high hopes of living to be brave men and worthy patriots; dear to God, and famous to all ages. —John Milton

Decided only to be undecided, resolved to be irresolute, adamant for drift, solid for fluidity, all-powerful to be impotent. —Winston Churchill

In peace, Love tunes the shepherd's reed;
In war, he mounts the warrior's steed;
In halls, in gay attire is seen;
In hamlets, dances on the green.

Love rules the court, the camp, the grove,
And men below, and saints above;
For love is heaven, and heaven is love.
—Sir Walter Scott, *Lay of the Last Minstrel*

Those bewigged ones, who are the performers, are so insufferably long in
their parts, so arrogant in their bearing, and so uninteresting in their
repetition, that you first admire, and then question, and at last execrate
the imperturbable patience of the judge. —Anthony Trollope, the *Palliser
Novels*

All our knowledge brings us nearer to our ignorance,
All our ignorance brings us nearer to death,
But nearness to death no nearer to God.
                    —T. S. Eliot

**B**DELYGMIA was called, not from the amphitheater, but from high overhead, so distant that I had not even noticed the spot she made in the sky. What came down in a dive, and landed with a thump before the Queen, was a vulture, with a naked neck and glittering gaze; her function in the Garden must have been to dispose of any animals that perished there. But when she bowed her horrid head, the Queen slipped the ribbon over it with grave courtesy, saying, "We owe you thanks, Bdelygmia." Then the vulture sang:

> I, Bdelygmia, shriek through
> The startled Garden, letting spew
> My imprecations on all who
>     May chance into my ken;
> "You spiteful, graceless, wormy beasts!
> You knaves, you rogues, you unfrocked priests!
> You customers of whores deceased!"
> And when you think I'm out of yeast,
>     I start to shriek again.

**Bdelygmia**   de LIG mee uh   (Gr. "abuse").
A litany of abuse.

If you are looking for ways to rail at someone, Bdelygmia is your bird. You will find her execrations scattered like droppings through literature. Try these for starters:

PRINCE *(Describing Sir John Falstaff):* Why dost thou converse with that trunk of humors, that bolting-hutch of beastliness, that swoln parcel of dropsies, that huge bombard of sack, that stuffed cloakbag of guts, that roasted Manningtree ox with the pudding in his belly, that reverend vice, that gray iniquity, that father ruffian, that vanity in years? —Shakespeare, *Henry IV*

OSWALD: What dost thou know me for?
KENT: A knave, a rascal, an eater of broken meats; a base, proud, shallow, beggarly, three-suited, hundred-pound, filthy, worsted-stocking knave; a lily-livered, action-taking, whoreson, glass-gazing, superserviceable, finical rogue; one-trunk-inheriting slave; one that wouldst be a bawd in way of good service, and art nothing but the composition of a knave, beggar, coward, pander, and the son and heir of a mongrel bitch; one whom I will beat into clamorous whining if thou deniest the least syllable of thy addition. —Shakespeare, *King Lear*

### The Curse

> Lord, confound this surly sister,
> Blight her brow with blotch and blister,
> Cramp her larynx, lung, and liver,
> In her guts a galling give her.

Let her live to earn her dinners
In Mountjoy with seedy sinners;
Lord, this judgment quickly bring,
And I'm your servant,
                                    —J. M. Synge

Mr. Lincoln evidently knows nothing of the higher elements of human nature. His soul seems made of leather, and incapable of any grand or noble
emotion. Compared with the mass of men, he is a line of flat prose in a
beautiful and spirited lyric. He lowers, he never elevates you . . . When he
hits upon a policy, substantially good in itself, he contrives to belittle it,
besmear it in some way to render it mean, contemptible and useless. Even
wisdom from him seems but folly. —*New York Post,* during the Civil War

A vile beastly rottenheaded foolbegotten brazenthroated pernicious piggish
screaming, tearing, roaring, perplexing, splitmecrackle crashmecriggle insane ass of a woman is practicing howling below-stairs with a brute of a
singingmaster so horribly, that my head is nearly off. —Edward Lear

The darling of feeble-minded royalty, the plaything of the camarilla, of the
court flunkeys covered with reptilian slime, and of the blasé hysterical female
court parasites who need this galvanic stimulation by massive instrumental
treatment to throw their pleasure-weary frog-legs into violent convulsion
. . . the diabolical din of this pig-headed man, stuffed with brass and sawdust,
inflated, in an insanely destructive self aggrandizement, by Mephistopheles'
mephitic and most venomous hellish miasma, into Beelzebub's Court Com-
poser and General Director of Hell's music. —*Wagner!*               —Klein

# DEFINITION UNPARALLELED

**Cactolith**
A quasi-horizontal chonolith composed of anastomising duc-
toliths, whose distal ends curl like a harpolith, thin like a spheno-
lith, or bulge discordantly like an akmolith or ethmolith.
                    —*Glossary of Geology and Related Sciences*
                       (American Geological Institute, 1957)

THOUGH to my certain knowledge the Gardener had been in his several parts exiled to my shed only a few hours before, and though he seemed to concede a relationship with me, even disrespectfully calling me pops, he nonetheless had inhabited the Garden since the sixteenth century, when it was created by Peacham. So, at least, insisted my neighbor the red imp. The only later arrival apart from me, said the imp, was the BOWDLER, which now came forward to be honored; it had been helping about the Garden for little more than a hundred and fifty years.

I call the Bowdler "it," for there was no way of judging its sex from its appearance. The body, disagreeably bloated, was swathed in a wrinkled black cloak that extended to the ground; the round face looked as if meant for merriment, but instead was set as if in pain. The Bowdler groaned all the way down the hill, continued groaning while its decoration was being hung, and still groaned between the lines as it sang:

> The Bowdler is a monster of a pitiable kind;
> > Its morals are extremely high, its
> > > thoughts extremely low;
>
> Indelicate allusions fan a fever in its mind,
> > But when it speaks, the worst it says is
> > > "Shoot," or "Gee," or "Oh."
>
> It's neither he nor she; it has no means of procreation;
> It tosses through the nighttime with unconsummated lust;
> It has no way to defecate, no hope of micturation;
> Its belly's mighty swollen, and someday it's bound to bust.

## Bowdlerism    BOHD luhr ism, BOUD luhr ism    (after Thomas Bowdler).
Prudish expurgation.

Dr. Thomas Bowdler brought out in 1818 a ten-volume edition of Shakespeare's works "in which nothing is added to the original text; but those words and expressions are omitted which cannot with propriety be read aloud in a family." He later performed the same service for Gibbon's *Decline and Fall of the Roman Empire*. *Bowdlerism* became a synonym for silly literary expurgations based on false modesty. The notion is generally out of style nowadays, except as the occasion for bad jokes; if Bowdler were around to purge the highly praised novels of our day, there would be no novels left.

More extreme than bowdlerism is censorship, which deletes instead of modifying. The ability of censorship to create obscenities out of air was

illustrated in the 1930s by a little red book called *Censored Mother Goose,*
which contained verses like this:

> Peter, Peter, pumpkin eater,
> Had a wife and couldn't [censored] her.
> He put her in a pumpkin shell
> And there he [censored] her very well.

THERE appeared on stage a picket fence, and on the fence rail a monstrous crow, as big as a tar barrel—no doubt the very crow that once frightened Tweedledum and Tweedledee out of fisticuffs. "I give you CATACHRESIS," said the Gardener. Apparently Catachresis was not popular in the Garden, for the audience broke into boos, hisses, honks, screams, whistles, and other sounds of disapproval. I inquired of the imp, raising my voice so that I could be heard above the hullabaloo:

"What do you all have against the crow?"

"He is sloppy at weeding, careless about fertilizing, and remiss about trimming," said the imp. "What is more, he hangs about with Acyrologia; we don't trust him. But occasionally he does develop some astonishingly beautiful hybrids; anyhow, the Queen thinks so; she won't hear a word against him."

The Gardener was waving his tongs vigorously for silence, and at length the booing died down. "Shame on you!" he cried. "Whom the Queen honors must be honored of us all!"

Catachresis cawed loudly as he flew down from his fence and approached the Queen. He fell silent only long enough for her to hang his award around his neck, and then he croaked his way through this song:

When Catachresis first heard poets puff,
    He found their figures weak.
He said, "They're not *conspicuous* enough—
    Come, speak the way *I* speak.
Dream up a simile that folks will note—
    That lingers in their ears."
("Indeed, indeed," said Thackeray, and wrote:
    "Earrings like chandeliers.")


**Catachresis**   ka tuh KREES is   (Gr. "misapplication").
An extreme metaphor; a strained or deliberately paradoxical figure of speech.

Catachresis may be the wrong use of one word for another, as *demean* for *debase, asset* for *advantage, conservative* for *low,* and *mutual* for *common.* It may be a metaphor made absurd by exaggeration. It may be a mixture of metaphors.

The British lion will never pull in its horns.
To take arms against a sea of troubles. —Shakespeare, *Hamlet*

Thus Sadat wrestled with the Devil for the soul of Egypt, and lost, because the Devil had most of the cards, and the jury of world opinion was half asleep and wholly blinkered. —Max Lerner, *New York Post*

Christian socialism is but the holy water with which the priest consecrates the heartburnings of the aristocrat. —Karl Marx

Every drop of ink in my pen ran cold. —Horace Walpole

Skewered through and through with office-pens, and bound hand and foot with red tape. —Charles Dickens

Experts can make catachresis into a powerful figure. But it is a mine-field; walk carefully, or you may be blown to bits.

**Homonym, Homophone**  HOM oh nim, HOM oh fohn  (Gr. "same name; same sound").

A word having the same pronunciation as another, but differing from it in origin, meaning, and, often, in spelling.

The following passage is from my *An Almanac of Words at Play:*

English contains homonyms by the thousands: *caul* and *call, hail* and *hale, pear* and *pair,* and the like. Many words have inner homonyms as well. Words within words may make an eerie kind of sense:

Compassion: come, passion. Purpose: purr, puss. Noble: no bull. Gasoline: Gas so lean. Diatribe: Die a tribe. Deplore: deep lore. Gruesome: grew some. Faltered: Fall turd. Freedom; free dumb. Junction: junk shun. Mission: miss shun. Section: sex shun. Lonesome: loan some. Shallow: shall owe. Kingdom: king dumb. Seeking: seek king. Kicking: kick king. Croaking: croak king. Promissory: promise, sorry. Polite: pole light. Horrid: whore id. Vowel: vow well. Tactile: tack tile. Sextant: sexed aunt. Succor: suck core. Thorax: Thor ax.

CATEGORIA was a cat, orange-colored, with a bushy tail; on his head was a plaid cap. He stood like a man, with one paw on a bag of golf clubs, as a hunter poses for his picture with his foot on the body of a slain lion. As he sang, he ticked off his points on his claws.

> You wonder why I will not play
> Another round with you today?
> Friend, listen well to what I say.
>
> You lie about your handicap;
> You tee your ball up in a trap;
> When I address my putt, you yap.
>
> You kick my ball behind a tree;
> You shoot a four and score it three;
> You let me pay the caddy fee.
>
> Your lack of moral discipline
> Has gotten underneath my skin;
> And, worst of all, you always win.

## Categoria   ka tuh GOR ee uh   (Gr. "accusation").
The direct exposure of an adversary's faults.

> Now when the even was come, he sat down with the twelve. And as they did eat, he said, Verily I say unto you, that one of you shall betray me. —Matthew 26: 20–21

> Here lie the remains of great Senator Vrooman,
> Whose head was as hard as the heart of a woman—
> Whose heart was as soft as the head of a hammer.
> Dame Fortune advanced him to eminence, d—— her.
> —Ambrose Bierce

> I said to my friend, "Joseph, I have always considered you a fine fellow. You lie on occasion, but who does not? You are not to be trusted with women, but who is? You are rascally in politics, but how else could you win elections? No, my only objection to you, Joseph, is that you are so infernally pleased with yourself." —W.R.E.

A plant broke through the wooden platform beside the throne and shot up to become an alder tree, and an aging one at that, for at once a yellowhammer was drilling into its trunk to find grubs in the rotting wood. He bored one hole after another, almost faster than the eye could follow, some angled up, some down, some to this side, some to that, until he had quite ringed the tree. There was a crunching sound, and the trunk began to break apart along the drill line; it leaned sidewise, then all at once crashed onto the stage, while the yellowhammer flew hastily aside, shouting, "Timber! Timber!" The Queen smiled, holding out her hand. "Come to me, COMMORATIO," she said, and the bird hopped cautiously forward, skirting the fallen tree as if fearing a branch might strike out at him. When the Queen had honored him, he flew to an upthrust branch, with the medal dangling from his neck, and sang:

> I, Commoratio, make each new hole a new surprise;
> The tree is felled before it's figured out the way I bore.
> So, too, when I my love for you would make you realize,
> I tell it not a single way but two or three or four:
> "I love your lips, I love your hair, I love your ears and eyes."
> Indeed I do; but ah! I love my variations more.

Then, wink-quick, the yellowhammer was gone, and the tree with him. The Gardener announced, "And now, Commoratio's dear friend— EXERGASIA!" An upright, opened umbrella was all at once on the stage; from the sky directly above it rain poured down, rattling on the umbrella top and pouring off the sides. "Dear Exergasia!" said the Queen, and arranged the ribbon of honor around the ferule at the umbrella's top; the rain separated so as not to touch her. The umbrella dipped in obeisance, hummed a moment to be sure it was on key, and sang this:

> The weather's simply horrible! The rain's
> Invading town in blankets, bedspreads, sheets;
> In cats, in dogs, balloons, and aeroplanes;
> In daisies, turnips, ravioli, beets.
>
> The rain's as endless as an argument,
> A headache, or a sermon, or a war;
> No rain like this has been since Noah sent
> His ark to sea—and no such rain before.

**Commoratio**   kah moh RAHT ee oh   (L. "dwelling").
The repetition of a point several times in different words.

· 78 ·

**Exergasia**   ek suhr GAHZ ee uh   (Gr. "working out").
The elaboration of a single idea in a series of figures of speech.

Commoratio is frequently encountered in the speeches of Cicero: "What didst thou covet? what didst thou wish? what didst thou desire?" Or again: "Thou hast abhorred thy parent, hated thy father, and despised him that begat thee."

This is exergasia, most commonly found in poetry:

> I take thy hand—this hand,
> As soft as dove's down and as white as it,
> Or Ethiopian's tooth, or the fann'd snow that's bolted
> By the northern blasts twice o'er.
>                                 —William Shakespeare

### Interminable names

The middle name of Dawne N. Lee, containing exactly one hundred letters, may be the longest Hawaiian name yet recorded. According to the November 8, 1967, issue of the *Honolulu Star-Bulletin,* the name is spelled as follows: Napaumohalaenaenaamekawehiwehionakuahiwiamenaawawakehoomakehoaalakeeaonaainananiakeaohawaiiikawanaao. The name means: "The fragrant abundant beautiful blossoms begin to fill the air of hills and valleys throughout the breadth and width of these glorious Hawaiian Islands at dawn."

The 1970 Dallas telephone directory listed a man with a surname forty-one letters long: Herbert Wolfeschlaegelsteinhausenbergerhaupfstedt.

CURTATIO was made like the Tin Man of Oz; he shone with a high polish. After receiving his medal, he leaned down and removed his feet. He then took off his legs below the knee; and then above the knee; and then set his torso aside; and then shrugged out of his arms. All these fell with a clang to the platform; but his tin head and oil can hat, ignoring gravity, rested on air while he sang this:

Do you recall, as I do,
    When words before anointment
Were weighed upon a hay scale
    To improve their embonpointment?

When words, like Gibson Girls, were
    Strategically plump,
And vied in beauty pageants
    For girth of bust or rump?

Ah, how I loved to watch them
    Come waddling down the lane:
*Quadrangle! Mobile vulgus!*
    *Fanatic! Aeroplane!*

And *Zoologic garden!*
    *Stenographer! Raccoon!*
*Stool pigeon! Schizophrenic!*
    *Detective! Pantaloon!*

*Vice-President!* and *Doctor!*
    *Biopsy! Autobus!*
*Professional!* And *Mamma!*
    And *Stradivarius!*

*Tricycle* and *Bicycle,*
    *Perambulator* too,
And even *Spatterdashes*
    Hove grandly into view.

But now the style's to diet;
    The pounds fall one by one;
Lo! yesterday's Fat Lady's
    Today's Live Skeleton—

A gaunt high-fashion model,
    The wraith of a gazelle;
What's in is see-through costumes
    And see-through words as well:

*Fan, Mob, Quad, Dick,* and *Stoolie;*
    *Plane, Steno, Zoo,* and *Bike;*
*Coon, Pants, Pro, Bus,* and *Bio;*
*Zoo, Doc, Ma, Strad,* and *Trike.*

Pert, plump *Perambulator*
Has shrunk to *Pram;* and what
Remains of *Spatterdashes?*
One lonely, mateless *Spat.*

## Curtatio   kor TAHT ee oh   (L. "shortened").
The shortening of words.

The word shortenings that take place under *aphaeresis, syncope, apocope,* and *synaloepha* (page 62), whether they occur at the beginning, middle, or end of a word, are also part of curtatio. *Mom* for *mama, pop* for *papa, drunk* for *drunkard, Gene* for *Eugene, Bill* for *William, taxi* (or *cab*) for *taxicab, e'er* for *ever, ne'er* for *never, quote* for *quotation, won't* for *will not, don't* for *do not*—these are curtatio. And so are the word changes in Curtatio's song: *fanatic* to *fan, mobile vulgus* to *mob, quadrangle* to *quad, aeroplane* to *plane, zoological garden* to *zoo, stenographer* to *steno, raccoon* to *coon, stool pigeon* to *stoolie,* and so on.

For cheating in an exam, the Princeton senior was denied a degree.
   —Newspaper story
I 'spect I growed. —Topsy in Harriet Beecher Stowe, *Uncle Tom's Cabin*

## Synonym   SIN oh nim   (Gr. "like name").
A word that shares one of its meanings with another word or words.

These words are synonomous with *street:*

alley · avenue · boulevard · Broadway · circle · court · crescent · drive · expressway · extension · freeway · highway · lane · line · market · midway · park · parkway · path · place · plaisance · plaza · road · skyway · square · terrace · throughway · tollway · way

**D**EHORTATIO was a bass fiddle, with spindly legs attached below and equally spindly arms above for stroking his bow across his strings. He sang a pantoum, to the accompaniment of groaning chords from his midsection:

> *Don't* teach egg-sucking to granny;
> *Don't* count your chickens unhatched;
> *Don't* take a nook for a cranny;
> *Don't* skin a badger uncatched.
>
> *Don't* count your chickens unhatched;
> *Don't* lament over spilled milk;
> *Don't* skin a badger uncatched;
> *Don't* mistake sow's ear for silk.
>
> *Don't* lament over spilled milk;
> *Don't* expect love ever true;
> *Don't* mistake sow's ear for silk;
> *Don't* mix "I don't" with "I do."
>
> *Don't* try to capture a star;
> *Don't* take a nook for a cranny;
> *Don't* try to walk in fresh tar;
> *Don't* teach egg-sucking to granny.

## Dehortatio    day hor TAHT ee oh    (L. "urging").
Dissuasive advice given with authority.

Dehortatio is negative persuasion: it tells what *not* to do, and sometimes gives reasons. This device is much less dangerous in argument than a knife or a gun. Cicero used it this way: "Never will or attempt that thing that cannot be. Also, for God's sake take heed, you judges, that through hope of present peace, you bring not in continual war and destruction."

Don't fire until you see the whites of their eyes. —Order to the American volunteers defending Bunker Hill in the opening battle of the Revolutionary War

Beware of all enterprises that require new clothes. —Henry David Thoreau

Thou shalt have no other gods before me. —First Commandment

Never give all the heart. —W. B. Yeats

Dost thou love life? Then do not squander time, for that is the stuff life is made of. —Benjamin Franklin

Don't repent so much—just don't sin so often. —Yiddish saying

Don't let's be beastly to the Germans. —Noel Coward

THE Gardener called for DIAERESIS and DIPHTHONG. There mounted to the stage two couples in ballet costume, the men in leotards and the women in tutus. They were slenderly and elegantly formed. The skin of the first pair was deeply black, the sort of blackness that seems to absorb the light striking it, while the other two had fair complexions and hair the color of dried hay. It appeared that none of the four had individual names; Diaeresis was applied jointly to the blacks, and Diphthong to the whites. Once the medals had been hung around their necks, they danced; there was music, but no sign of the orchestra.

Though the two couples moved to the same beat, their actions conveyed opposite messages. When one of the Diaeresis pair tried to touch the other, both instead leaped back, repelled as if both were charged with positive electricity. The dance of the Diphthongs, on the other hand, was a whirl of caressing, kissing, and clinging, as if the two sought to merge into one before our eyes. When the dance was over, and the applause had died down, the two couples sang these songs:

*Diphthong:*
Vowels we, in Diphthong mated,
Each in each incorporated:
*Boy* and *out* and *coin* and *how,*
*Soil* and *round* and *boil* and *vow.*
Pity we in nuptial bed
Vowels that refuse to wed!

*Diaeresis:*
Diaretic vowels, quite
Opposite, will not unite.
Caught in contigu*i*ty
Though by evil chance we be,
Thrust together loin to loin,
Yet we will not kiss and join.

Love we find invid*ious,*
Coos and kisses hid*eous.*
Hear us say zoölogy—
Bia s—rio t—poe try—
Keeping, spite of all temptations,
Separate pronunciations.


**Diaeresis**   dī AR uh sis   (Gr. "taking asunder").
The pronunciation of two adjoining vowels in a word as separate sounds.

**Diphthong**   DIF thong   (Gr. "two voices").
A sound beginning with one vowel sound and moving to another, or joining to form a single sound.

Some diaereses:

Incestuous · Residual · Chaos · Poet · Paleontology · Biology · Diabolic · Idea · Idiot · Diary · Chloe · Sobriety · Society · Experience · Insouciance · Coitus · Perpetuate · Bias · Riot · Aerated

As most commonly thought of, a diphthong consists of adjoining vowels with sounds that fade into each other: *oi* as in c*oi*n, j*oi*n, f*oi*l, b*oi*l; *ou* as in c*ou*ch, *ou*ch, r*ou*t, st*ou*t. But *ā*, *ī*, *ō*, and *ū* are diphthongs too; listen as you enunciate them, and you will see that *ā* and *ī* end in the sound of *e,* and *ō* in the sound of *ōō*, while *ū* begins with the sound of *y*.

# Similes*

As wet as a fish—as dry as a bone;
As live as a bird—as dead as a stone;
As plump as a partridge—as poor as a rat;
As strong as a horse—as weak as a cat;
As hard as a flint—as soft as a mole;
As white as a lily—as black as a coal;
As plain as a pike-staff—as rough as a bear;
As light as a drum—as free as the air;
As heavy as lead—as light as a feather;
As steady as time—uncertain as weather;
As hot as an oven—as cold as a frog;
As gay as a lark—as sick as a dog;
As slow as the tortoise—as swift as the wind;
As true as the Gospel—as false as mankind;
As thin as a herring—as fat as a pig;
As proud as a peacock—as blithe as a grig;
As savage as tigers—as mild as a dove;
As stiff as a poker—as limp as a glove;
As blind as a bat—as deaf as a post;
As cool as a cucumber—as warm as a toast;
As flat as a flounder—as round as a ball;
As blunt as a hammer—as sharp as an awl;
As red as a ferret—as safe as the stocks;
As bold as a thief—as sly as a fox;
As straight as an arrow—as crook'd as a bow;
As yellow as saffron—as black as a sloe;
As brittle as glass—as tough as a gristle;
As neat as my nail—as clean as a whistle;
As good as a feast—as bad as a witch;
As light as is day—as dark as is pitch;
As brisk as a bee—as dull as an ass;
As full as a tick—as solid as brass.

—Anonymous

*And they're clichés, too.

**D**ICAEOLOGIA was a weasel, mean and furtive-looking. It puzzled me that the Queen had chosen him to honor. He sneered as he accepted his medal. The song he sang was called "If It Hadn't Been for You":

> I never would have done it if it hadn't been for you:
> I never would have beat my horse, or even kicked the dog;
> I never would have driven drunk, or raised a foofaroo;
> I never would have.
>
> I never would have robbed that church, or burned that synagogue;
> I never would have told that lie, or throttled that emu;
> I never would have cut that tree, or drowned that polliwog;
> I never would have.
>
> I never would have kept on doing things I shouldn't do;
> I never would have kissed your wife, or played the demagogue;
> I never would have pushed my uncle Andy in the slough.
> I never would have.

**Dicaeologia**   di see AHL oh jee uh   (Gr. "discourse").
The device of defending an act with excuses.

This human habit began with Adam and Eve. Caught fig-leafed after they had eaten the apple, Adam justified himself by saying: "The woman whom thou gavest to be with me, she gave me of the tree, and I did eat." Eve, in turn, explained: "The serpent beguiled me."

We have been making excuses ever since. Peacham gives examples: "I foresook my friend, but the laws compelled me." "I have done amiss, but consider I was a young man and conversant among those by whom I could not choose but be corrupted."

And so on and on: I overslept, I had a headache, I didn't think you cared, the other car cut into my lane, I mistook you for somebody else, I didn't have time to learn my lines.

If we had to label all our excuses "dicaeologia" we might not make so many of them. It is a hard word to pronounce.

T HE Gardener called, "Ellipsis!" A garden rake scuttled past me, handle upright and tines at the bottom. He moved with considerable agility in view of the necessity to first move forward the tines on one side, and then those on the other. The tines gathered up cut hay as they went, leaving it behind in neat little haycocks. Ellipsis's head was a scarcely discernible swelling at the top of his handle, so when the Queen first draped his medal, it slid down to the bottom; she solved the problem by tying the ribbon tight about his middle.

This was the song that Ellipsis sang:

Ellipsis was a wicked boy, Ellipsis was a rake;
Ellipsis was an implement forever on the make.
Ellipsis met a maiden scythe residing in a cart;
Her blade was bright, her edge was sharp, her curves perturbed his heart.
He spoke to her in rakish tones, she gathered his intent;
It didn't matter what he said, she knew just what he meant.
She said, "I will not have it, sir, I pray you go away";
He'd scarcely drawn the curtain up, but she knew all the play.
Yet they were wedded in the end, and live in manner blithe;
Their baby boy is half a rake and half a haying scythe.
And when he cries by day or night, which frequently occurs,
Although he cannot speak they know he needs dry diapers.

**Ellipsis**   e LIP sis   (Gr. "a falling short").
A figure by which one or more words are omitted, which are to be supplied by the listener or reader.

Ellipses are so pervasive in language that they are seldom noticed. In both speech and writing, we assume a common background of knowledge that does not have to be explained. Take this clerihew by E. C. Bentley:

When Alexander Pope
Stepped on the soap
And fell on his head
Never mind what he said.

Mr. Bentley assumed that his readers would know Pope as the great neoclassicist poet of the eighteenth century. He assumed they would understand also that when he stepped on the soap he was in the shower (though probably Mr. Pope was unfamiliar with that way of bathing), and that the soap must have slipped from his hands as he was scrubbing himself. And they would be well aware that whatever he said, it was not polite.

The woods are lovely, dark and deep,
But I have promises to keep,
And miles to go before I sleep.
                    —Robert Frost, "Stopping by Woods on a Snowy Evening"

Men who cherish for women the highest respect are seldom popular with.
                    —Joseph Addison

Everybody's friend is nobody's.
                    —Arthur Schopenhauer

If youth knew, if age could.
                    —Henri Estienne, 16th century

Familiar speech is peppered with ellipses:

"Stop crying!" for "You stop crying!"
"People I like" for "People whom I like"
"The hits he made" for "The hits which he made"
"Let him out" for "Let him go out"
"Let him in" for "Let him come in"
"She looked fat" for "She looked to be fat"

**Brachylogy**  bra KIL uh jee  (Gr. "short speech").
Irregular shortening down of expression. A kind of ellipsis.

Technically, you should not say, "I want less salt." You
should say, "I want less of salt." Technically, you should not say,
"This is no use." You should say, "This is of no use." Nor should
you say, "A is as good or better than B." You should say, "A is
as good as or better than B."

Look for further examples under *ellipsis* (page 88).

**T**HE Gardener called ENANTIOSIS, who was as shifty as Antithesis—now an angel, with white feathered wings; now a devil,
with horns and a forked tail. Devil or angel, Enantiosis was
duly honored, and in gratitude sang a triolet and another
song, changing back and forth from bass to falsetto:

> If love be fine, as some pretend,
> The lady's not for burning.
> What blame is here who love doth lend
> If love be fine, as some pretend?
> The sin is when the kisses end—
> The fault in love is spurning.
> If love be fine, as some pretend,
> The lady's not for burning.

The second song was a string of unconnected observations:

> You say old age is hard to live?
> Consider the alternative!

> She found no hair on his lapel,
> And charged, "You date bald girls as well!"

> The wheat's not better than the chaff?
> Oh, no, it's not—oh, no—not half!

## Enantiosis   en an ti OHS is   (Gr. "contradiction").

A negative statement of what is to be understood affirmatively, or vice
versa.

Enantiosis is rather arch:

Oh, no, *she* doesn't like the boys. Oh, no! Not her!
Sure, he's just a *little* geezer. Six feet six—that's all *he* is.

T HE difference between EPIZEUXIS and a magnified bumblebee was that Epizeuxis sported not one but three sets of wings. They turned the air around him into a golden blur. He flew to the stage, humming so loudly that I put my hands over my ears.

This was his thank-you song to the Queen:

Epizeuxis' emphasis is queer, queer, *queer;*
   He doesn't fly on wings alone, but wings, wings, *wings;*
The stinger in his rear is in his rear, rear, *rear;*
He's not content to sting you once, he stings, stings, *stings.*

**Epizeuxis**    ep i ZOOK sis    (Gr. "a fastening together").
The repetition of a word for emphasis.

We are likely to use epizeuxis in moments of stress, for lack of a quick synonym. "Oh you, oh you, oh you," a lover may say, finding further elucidation quite beyond his powers of expression.

America, America, God shed his grace on thee. —Katharine Lee Bates

Corydon, Corydon, what madness hath thee moved? —Virgil

O earth, earth, earth, hear the word of the Lord. —Jeremiah 22:29

O my son Absalom, my son, my son Absalom! would God I had died for thee,
   O Absalom, my son, my son. —2 Samuel 18:33.

Break, break, break
On thy cold gray stones, O Sea! —Tennyson, "Break, Break, Break"

Blow, bugle, blow, set the wild echoes flying.
Blow, bugle; answer, echoes, dying, dying, dying. —Tennyson, *The Princess*

Keeping time, time, time,
In a sort of Runic rhyme,
To the tintinnabulation that so musically wells
From the bells, bells, bells, bells, bells, bells, bells. —Edgar Allan Poe, "The Bells"

True education makes for inequality; the inequality of individuality, the inequality of success; the glorious inequality of talent, of genius; for inequality, not mediocrity, individual superiority, not standardization, is the measure of the progress of the world. —F. Schelling

Curiosity is almost, almost, the definition of frivolity. —Ortega y Gasset

A repetition broken up by one or more intervening words is called not epizeuxis but *diacope*  dī AK oh pee  (Gr. "a cutting in two") or *tmesis* (page 142). Thus, Shakespeare has Richard cry: "A horse! a horse! my kingdom for a horse!" Hamlet exclaims: "O villain, villain, smiling, smiling villain!"

**Tom Swifty**
A device of word play in which an adverb puns on a noun.

Tom Swift, hero of a series of novels once extremely popular with boys, was a youthful genius who invented such wonders as electric airplanes. The books are out of vogue now, but the punning word game named in Tom's honor is still going strong. These Tom Swifties will give you the idea:

"He's a young M.D.," said Tom internally.
"You gave me two less than a dozen," said Tom tensely.
"Gold leaf," said Tom guiltily.
"I have the mumps," said Tom infectiously.
"Shirtwaist," said Tom blowsily.
"Our ball club needs a man who can hit sixty homers a season," said Tom ruthlessly.
"Maid's night off," said Tom helplessly.
"I don't like wilted lettuce," said Tom limply.
"Pass the cards," said Tom ideally.
"I'm out of cartridges for my starting gun," said Tom blankly.
"Zero," said Tom naughtily.
"I'm afraid prunes aren't my dish," said Tom loosely.

Mr. and Mrs. Roy Bongartz developed Croakers, a variant of Tom Swifties in which a verb rather than an adverb provides the pun:

"I spent the day sewing and gardening," she hemmed and hawed.
"The fire is going out," he bellowed.
"You can't really train a beagle," he dogmatized.
"I've got a new game," mumbled Peg.
"I used to be a pilot," he explained.

EUPHEMISM wore a mask, so that I could not make out his features; he seemed a decent sort, and I did not understand why he wished to hide his face. His song to the Queen ran this way:

Euphemism never lies, though some will tell you so;
Though he may say "pass on" for "die," he knows you really *know;*
You know a rest room's more than *that,* and so's "Let's go to bed";
You know that "plumpish" stands for "fat," and "We-ell" means "Come
    ahead."
Mischance befell a sweet young thing, who euphemized as you do;
"Oh, shit!" she said to mama. "I have stepped into some doodoo."

## Euphemism   YŌOF uhm ism   (Gr. "use of good words").

Decorous speech; the substitution of an inoffensive term for one considered offensively explicit.

It is hard to face facts; I for one frequently prefer to evade them. The Greeks described as Eumenides—"gracious ones"—the snake-haired avenging deities who visit retribution on those who have committed unforgivable crimes. This effort to propitiate the agents of justice, evil, or misfortune by giving them innocuous names continues to this day; it is as old as speech, and as new as tomorrow's newspaper. Hugh Rawson has brought out a book on euphemisms,* of which these are a fragmentary sampling:

> *Covering one's feet:* an ancient Hebrew euphemism for the relieving of the
>     bowels. "And he came to the sheep-cotes by the way, where was a cave,
>     and Saul went in to cover his feet."
> *Fertilizer* for *manure; manure* for *shit.*
> *Indisposed* for sick.
> *Inexpressibles* for *underwear.*
> *Pass away, expire, breathe one's last,* for *die.*
> *Know:* Biblical euphemism for "have sexual intercourse."

Howard Bergerson, in *Word Ways,* cites these evolving euphemisms:

> *Tumor* becomes *cancer* becomes *growth.*
> *Backward* (in intelligence) becomes *retarded* becomes *exceptional.*
> *Bowels* become *guts* become *intestines* become *viscera.*
> *Lunacy* becomes *insanity* becomes *psychosis* becomes *emotional illness* becomes
>     *disturbance.*
> *Madhouse* becomes *insane asylum* becomes *mental hospital* becomes *psychiatric*
>     *hospital* becomes *sanitarium.*

*\*Dictionary of Euphemisms and Other Double Talk* (New York: Crown, 1981).

EXAGGERATIO, a frog, was called, and came to the stage hopping. She wore a pair of horn-rimmed spectacles with magnifying lenses, so that her eyes seemed as big as dinner plates. After receiving her medal, Exaggeratio drew in her breath until she began to swell like a child's balloon when air is blown into it. I feared she might burst, like the ambitious frog in the fable; but at length the inhalation ceased. Air sighed from her mouth as she sang in a resonant croak:

> An itty-bitty pondfrog (being told
>  A nearby bull was bigger)
> Breathed in so deeply that her body swolled
>  An itty-bitty.
>
> "No bull alive," she cried, "can match my figger!
>  I've got him beaten cold!
> You claim he's big as this? You make me snigger
>  An itty-bitty."
>
> The bull came by to drink, and being old
>  And dim-eyed, chanced to swig her.
> Her size compared to his she'd overtold
>  An itty-bitty.

## Exaggeratio   eg zaj uh RAHT ee oh   (L. "piling up").
Overstatement; magnification beyond the truth.

We all know those who, if a person is comfortably off, will insist he is a millionaire; if he is six feet tall, will make him six and a half; if he has caught a cold, will have him dying of pneumonia. Exaggeration is so common a part of daily conversation that we automatically discount some statements; the only question is how great a percentage the discount shall be.

> You might have heard a pin fall—a pin! a feather! —Charles Dickens, *Nicholas Nickleby*

> In Köln, a town of monks and bones,
> And pavements fanged with murderous stones
> And rags, and hags, and hideous wenches,
> I counted two and seventy stenches,
> All well defined, and several stinks! —Samuel Taylor Coleridge, "Cologne"

> "Heat, ma'am!" I said; "it was so dreadful here, that I found there was nothing left for it but to take off my flesh and sit in my bones." —Sydney Smith

Bdelygmia and exaggeration frequently overlap:

Thy skin is like an unwasht carrot's,
Thy tongue is blacker than a parrot's,
Thy teeth are crooked, but belong
Inherently to such a tongue. —Walter Savage Landor

HYPERBOLE was lovelier than Hera, Athene, Aphrodite, and Helen combined. To be sure, I have not been so fortunate as to see those four rival beauties, but I saw Hyperbole close when she passed me on her way to be decorated, and I was able to examine her judiciously, since she walked with slow grace, pleased to be admired, and wore no more than did Aphrodite when she first arose from the sea. Only the Queen herself was as fair. When she sang, my heart turned over at the glory of the sound. These are the words:

> Hyperbole speaks not amiss.
> > Though she may seem to overstate,
> It's just her way of emphasis.
>
> She sighs, "I perish for your kiss."
> > That's not exactly so—but wait;
> Hyperbole speaks not amiss.
>
> "No mortal ever knew such bliss,"
> > She whispers. Fool, do not debate—
> It's just her way of emphasis.
>
> "None ever knew such love as this,"
> > She sighs. Don't question—consummate!
> Hyperbole speaks not amiss.
>
> She's really *not* in the abyss,
> > Or hovering at heaven's gate—
> It's just her way of emphasis.
>
> Yet she speaks not in artifice;
> > Her words do not dissimulate.
> Hyperbole speaks not amiss—
> It's just her way of emphasis.

## Hyperbole  hī PUHR boh lee  (Gr. "excess").
An extravagant statement used as a figure of speech.

Hyperbole, the boldest figure of rhetoric, enables us to describe what otherwise would be beyond description. "A wicked man," says Peacham, "is wickedness personified; a virtuous man, virtue come to life. This one is more blind than blindness, that one more vain than vanity. Sweetness is sweeter than honey, bitterness more bitter than gall. Or the comparison may be with living creatures: swifter than the swallow; blacker than the crow. Or with the gods and goddesses: more beautiful than Venus; mightier than Mars. Or with characters of myth: wearier than Sisyphus; thirstier than Tantalus. Or of history: richer than Croesus. Or offices: more stately than an emperor; more hated than a hangman."

I could sleep all year.
His face would stop a clock.
This book weighs a ton.

                       I would
Love you ten years before the Flood;
And you should, if you please, refuse
Till the conversion of the Jews.
My vegetable love should grow
Vaster than empires and more slow.
—Andrew Marvell, "To His Coy Mistress"

Publishing a volume of verse is like dropping a rose-petal down the Grand
    Canyon and waiting for the echo. —Don Marquis
In America [writes an Englishman] things seem rather larger than life. I have
    just received a kind invitation to a Medical Alumni Social Hour; it is from
    6 to 8 P.M.

## Doublet

The change of a word into its opposite by substituting one letter
at a time without changing the order of the others, each change
creating another word. The game was popularized by Lewis Car-
roll, who gave it its name.

*Sober to drunk* in thirteen steps: *sober, saber, saver, paver, paves, pales, palls,
pails, pains, paint, print, prink, drink, drunk.*—Harriet B. Naughton, in
*Word Ways*
*Sober* to *drunk* in nine steps: *sober, sorer, sores, cores, corns, coins, crins, crink,
drink, drunk.* (*Crins* are heavy silk substances prepared from the con-
tents of a silkworm's glands. *Crink* is a verb meaning "to make a thin,
metallic, or cracking sound.")—Darryl H. Francis, in *Word Ways*

CAME the turn of HYPOCORE, a panda who looked as soft and yielding as a pillow; I restrained an impulse—and so, I am sure, did every other member of the audience—to rush forward and cuddle her. She accepted her decoration, and sang a sonnet:

> Hail now the goddess of pet words, whose laws
>     Rule sweet exchanges tying Him to Her!
> Hypocore is soft of gaze; her fur
>     Soft, too, and good to stroke on; and her paws
> Soft, soft for petting, with retracted claws.
>     Her voice is softer than a kitten's purr,
>     Her smile as sweet as ever candies were;
> And soft, soft, soft the breath she draws, withdraws.
>
> "Duck, darling, dove"—so she addresses you;
>     "My sweet, my doll, my dumpling, my delight,
> My love, my sugarplum, my kitchy-koo;
>     My sun in daytime, and my moon at night!"
>
> (Yet I grow wary when in accents sweet
> She tells me I am good enough to eat.)

**Hypocore**   hī PAHK oh ree   (Gr. "playing the child").
The use of pet names and names of endearment.

*Harry* for *Henry, Dick* for *Richard, Molly* for *Mary, Lizzy* or *Beth* for *Elizabeth, hankie* for *handkerchief, frillies* for *underwear*—these are hypocore no less than are lovers' exchanges.

MOZART: Who am I? . . . Quick: tell me. Hold me and tell who I am. Who?
    —come on.
CONSTANZE: Pussy-wussy.
MOZART: Who else?
CONSTANZE: Miaowy-powy.
MOZART: And you're squeaky-peeky. And Stanzi-manzi. And Bini-gini!
    *(She surrenders.)*
CONSTANZE: Wolfi-polfi!
MOZART: Poopy-peepee!
    *(They giggle.)*
CONSTANZE: Now don't be stupid.
MOZART *(Insistent: like a child):* Come on—do it. Do it. . . . Let's do it. "Poppy."
    *(They play a private game, gradually
    doing it faster, on their knees.)*
CONSTANZE: Poppy.
MOZART *(Changing it):* Pappy.
CONSTANZE *(Copying):* Pappy.

MOZART: Pappa.
CONSTANZE: Pappa.
MOZART: Pappa-pappa!
CONSTANZE: Pappa-pappa!
MOZART: Pappa-pappa-pappa-pappa!
CONSTANZE: Pappa-pappa-pappa-pappa!
  *(They rub noses.)*
TOGETHER: Pappa-pappa-pappa-pappa! Pappa-pappa-pappa-pappa!
  —Peter Shaffer, *Amadeus*

**Heteronym**   HET uhr uh nym   (Gr. "different law").
A word identical in spelling but different in sound and meaning
from another.

>  *Row* (roh): a series. *Row* (row): a fight.
>  *Sow* (sow): a pig. *Sow* (soh): to strew seeds.
>  *Polish* (PAH lish): to make smooth and shiny. *Polish* (POH lish):
>    pertaining to Poland.
>  *Entrance* (EN trans): a passage affording entry. *Entrance* (en TRANS):
>    to put into a trance.
>  *Present* (PREZ ent): the present time. *Present* (pri ZENT): to introduce,
>    offer.
>  *Content* (kuhn TENT): satisfied. *Content* (KAHN tent): that which is
>    contained.
>  *Intimate* (IN ti MAYT): to imply subtly. *Intimate* (IN ti mit): marked
>    by close acquaintance.
>  *Agape* (a GAYP): in a state of amazement, often with the mouth wide
>    open. *Agape* (AH gah pay): Christian love.

**H**YSTERON PROTERON was clearly a horse, but an odd one. She walked backward to the stage, and it quickly became evident that her mouth performed the functions usually associated with a horse's other end, and vice versa. The other end sang this:

> Hysteron Proteron, backward inclined:
> Hindermost forwardmost, foremost behind;
> "You have grown mighty, and soon will be strong";
> "You are mistaken, and soon will be wrong";
> "Mother, you reared me, and bore me also";
> "Let us die nobly, and plunge on the foe";
> "Surely you love me, I know that you will";
> "Jack and Jill tumbled, and climbed up the hill";
> "Soon we shall marry, and first we'll divorce"—
> Topsy is turvy, and cart precedes horse.

## Hysteron proteron    HIS tor ahn PROH tor ahn    (Gr. "hinder foremost").

A figure of speech in which the word that should come last is placed first.

The suspect was charged with murder and rape.

The new drug will ward off death and heart attacks.

*Valet atque vivit.* (He is well, and also lives.)

He was bred and born a gentleman.

*Moriamur, et in media arma ruamus.* (Let us die, and rush into the midst of the fray.) —Virgil

Masters, it is proved already that you are little better than false knaves, and it will go near to be thought so shortly. —Dogberry in Shakespeare, *Much Ado About Nothing*

Th'Antoniad, the Egyptian admiral, with all their sixty, fly and turn the rudder. —Shakespeare, *Antony and Cleopatra*

**Acrostic**  a KROS tik  (Gr. "end-line").

A composition, usually in verse, in which one or more sets of letters, as the initial or final letters of the lines, taken in sequence, form a word or words.

Solve this acrostic by taking in order the initial letters of the lines:

### In God We Trust

Insane titterings heard on the stair,
Nightmarish shadows thrown on the wall,
Grim windless blasts felt in the old hall,
Odd ghosts invade my sick mind and soul.
Daily I ail with a strange malaise;
Wild with terror, my lovely Gervaise
Entreats we leave while my mind is whole.
Taut with fear I search this haunted pile,
Roaring her name, but Gervaise has fled.
Unless . . . Why is my hand stained this red?
Sadly I recall her tortured smile
That now fills my heart with dark despair.
       —Walter Shedlofsky, in *Word Ways*

To read the message hidden in the verse below, replace the first letter of each line with the letter that precedes it in the alphabet:

### Song for a Season

Now, a little while,
   From the care and cark,
Something like a smile
   Shimmers in the dark.

Zephyr's scented art
   Dwindles rime and snow;
In a melted heart,
   Softly, flowers grow.

Joy, a moment now,
   Thumps old Sorrow's side;
Under festive bough
   Nemesis has died.

Brief, by iron laws,
   Though this magic be,
Unbeliever, pause;
   Pagan, bend your knee.

Zest as keen as this
   Pricks the sullen soul;
Vast polarities
   Blend in vaster whole.

Mark—the night is through.
Memory must do.
       —W.R.E.

WHEN the Gardener announced, "IRONIA!" up sprang none other than my friend the red imp, who cartwheeled down the hill, with his forked tail held rigid so that at the completion of each flip he landed on his tines instead of his feet. Once decorated, he placed a monocle in his right eye, arranged his features in an expression of disdain, and sang:

> My name is Irony. I sing
>    Of darkness to evoke the dawn;
> Of winter, understanding spring;
>    And childhood, meaning age comes on;
>
> *Sing: "Poor and rich have equal right*
> *To sleep beneath a bridge at night";*
>
> *Sing: "Give up women? That's no sweat—*
> *I have before, and I will yet."*
>
> My name is Irony. If you
>    Think yes and no must disagree,
> I'm sure you're right, and stout, and true—
>    But stay away from Irony.

His second song was a limerick:

> Bob Benchley, fatigued at a play,
> Protested, while slipping away,
>    "They've ruined the spell
>    By *pronouncing* too well;
> You can hear every word that they say."

## Ironia   ī ROHN ee uh   (Gr. "dissembler").

The use of words to convey the opposite of their literal meaning; covert sarcasm.

The word *irony* came into use to describe a trick of Socrates, who in order to expose the ignorance of an opponent would pretend to seek instruction from him. The unwary may fail to perceive the intended meaning of an ironic utterance under the apparent one.

> A drayman, in a passion, calls out, "You are a pretty fellow," without suspecting that he is uttering irony. —Thomas B. Macaulay
> He said he considered £40,000 a year a moderate income—such a one as a man might jog on with. —William James Lampton
> Marriage: The state or condition of a community consisting of a master, a mistress and two slaves, making in all two. —Ambrose Bierce
> He [Macaulay] has occasional flashes of silence that make his conversation perfectly delightful. —Sydney Smith

Armaments, universal debt and planned obsolescence—those are the three
  pillars of Western prosperity. —Aldous Huxley
Have not the Indians been kindly and justly treated? Have not the temporal
  things, the vain baubles and filthy lucre of this world, which were too apt
  to engage their worldly and selfish thought, been benevolently taken from
  them? And have they not instead thereof, been taught to set their affection
  on things above? —Washington Irving
There are not ten writers in Boston equal to Shakespeare. —Unknown

HE red imp returned to his place at my side, looking well pleased with himself, and was followed by KLIMAX, a string of six green grasshoppers in single file. They proceeded down the hill and up to the stage in this wise: the first five remained motionless while the sixth leapfrogged over them to become the foremost; then again the hindmost leapfrogged the line; and so on until they were gathered around the Queen, who gave each a kind word and a decoration. They then arranged themselves in a pyramid, with three grasshoppers forming the base, two standing on the three, and one on the two. The pyramid chirped:

> I pray, God, I may never wed;
> But if thou grant this not, instead
> I pray that in my misery
> At least I not cuckolded be.
> If this plea too thou must refuse,
> I pray I never hear the news.
> If thou deny this final prayer,
> I pray I may have ceased to care.*

## Klimax   KLĪM aks   (Gr. "ladder").
A series of statements in an ascending order of intensity.

Klimax (climax) is exemplified in 1 Corinthians 2:9: "[1] Eye hath not seen, [2] nor ear heard, [3] neither have entered into the heart of man, [4] the things which God hath prepared . . ."

What is climactic, what is anticlimactic, what is mere progression, is as much the decision of the reader as the intention of the writer. The rhetorical device runs along these lines:

> There was too much spice where there should be none; there was sogginess where crispness was all-important; there was an artificially whipped and heavily sweetened canned-milk dessert where nothing at all was wanted.
> —M. F. K. Fisher

> Cromwell was bold when he closed the Long Parliament. Shaftesbury was bold when he formed the plot for which Lord Russell and others suffered. Walpole was bold when, in his lust for power, he discarded one political friend after another. And Peel was bold when he resolved to repeal the Corn Laws. But in none of these instances was the audacity displayed more wonderful than when Mr. Daubeny took upon himself to make known throughout the country his intention of abolishing the Church of England.
> —Trollope, *Phineas Redux*

> I would be absolute; and who but I? Now, he that is absolute can do what he likes; he that can do what he likes, can take his pleasure; he that can take his pleasure, can be content; and he that can be content, has nought to desire. —Cervantes, *Don Quixote*

*My variant on "The Bachelor's Prayer," which dates from 1630.

**L**ITOTES was now summoned. I noted that Litotes was not plump, not short, not ugly, not solemn, not bad to look at, and not male. This was her song:*

> The shy, elusive Lit-o-tes
>> Is not a cinch to spot;
> For Lit-o-tes one never sees—
>> One sees what she is *not:*
>> Not crook; not fool; not sot;
> Not small event; not great affair;
>> Not easily forgot.
> You'll find, when Lit-o-tes you snare,
> Her opposite is really there.

## Litotes   LIT oh teez   (Gr. "simple; plain; unadorned").
The expression of an affirmative by the negation of its opposite.

Litotes, like Antithesis and Enantiosis, speaks in negatives. But where Antithesis balances one idea against its opposite, and Enantiosis states a negative so as to imply an affirmative, Litotes deduces the affirmative from the proposition that its opposite is not so: "I kid you not," Jack Parr regularly assured his viewers on the *Tonight* television show, meaning that he was telling no more and no less than the truth.

> The Ayrshire grouse-shooting is not the best in Scotland, but the shooting in the Portray mountains is not the worst shooting in the county.
> —Trollope, *The Eustace Diamonds*
> It was not our finest hour. —Ambassador William Sullivan, referring to the takeover of the American embassy in Teheran by an Iranian mob
> The magazine has not been known for the punctuality of its appearances.
> —George Plimpton, speaking of the *Paris Review*
> Mr. Harriman is not exactly a Horatio Alger rags-to-riches character.
> —James Reston on Averell Harriman, a politician-statesman of inherited wealth

> Not bad, eh?  ·  Not a few  ·  He does not starve himself  ·  It was no small task  ·  She was no country cousin  ·  It is not unusual  ·  This is no small problem  ·  A citizen of no mean city  ·  No dwarf of a man

---

*It is along the lines of a Spenserian stanza.

**M**ETAPHORA was an owl with eyes the size of dinner plates. Each of them presented moving images, like a television tube; and there was no relation between the events in one eye and the other. When the owl blinked, the images changed channels.

Metaphora accepted his medal, and sang:

> A Simile is prudent how he goes;
> He takes out chosen parts of these and those.
> He's sour as garden greens, but he's not greens;
> He's tight as custom jeans, but he's not jeans.
>
> I, Metaphor, take all, from bone to skin:
> "Time's but the stream I go a-fishing in . . ."
> "There is a tide in the affairs of men . . ."
> I am all things; all things are me again.

**Metaphora**   me TAF or ah   (Gr. "transference").
The transfer of properties of one thing, idea, image, or event to another in speech or writing.

Fowler divides metaphors between the quick and the dead. The quick are those accepted in awareness that they are substitutes for their living equivalents; the dead are those so familiar that we no longer realize that the words used are not literal. *Sift* is a live metaphor in "Satan hath desired to have you, that he may sift you as wheat." But in "the sifting of evidence," the metaphor is so familiar that it is dormant, if not dead; it does not give rise to an image of *sieve* at all.

By means of metaphor we express the otherwise inexpressible. The modern fashion is to keep the figure short and clear, though at one time writers hung their metaphors one after the other like strings on a bead. The eighteenth-century English novelist Samuel Richardson wrote:

> Tost to and fro by the high winds of passionate control, I behold the desired port, the single state, into which I would fain enter; but am kept off by the foaming billows of a brother's and sister's envy, and by the raging winds of a supposed invaded authority; while I see in Lovelace, the rocks on one hand, and in Solmes, the sands on the other; and tremble, lest I should split upon the former or strike upon the latter.

As a generalization (with many exceptions), a simile, which is an avowed comparison, is decorative, while a metaphor, in which the comparison is implicit, is practical, intended to make a point in the most effective possible way. A simile often includes many points of reference;

a metaphor is frequently expressed in but one—"if ye had not plowed with my heifer," for instance, meaning "slept with my wife."

> Now is the winter of our discontent / Made glorious summer by this sun of York. —Shakespeare, *Richard III*
>
> It being a windy day, half a dozen men were tacking across the road. —Charles Dickens, *Nicholas Nickleby*
>
> A bad-tempered elbow —V. S. Pritchett, *A Cab at the Door*
>
> The salivating torments of anticipation and the long, rich pastures of neglect. —Peter Dickinson, *The Lively Dead*
>
> An event so electric with comedy that it has been stubbornly settled in my mind ever since, a lodger refusing to gather up its hat and go. —John Wolcott
>
> Now he was a broken-down old man—whose mind had been, as it were, unbooted and put into moral slippers for the remainder of its term of existence upon earth. —Anthony Trollope, the Palliser novels

> He bridles his anger · Don't count your chickens before they are hatched · That's a horse of a different color · Crocodile tears · Wildcat strike · Take the bull by the horns · Bite the bullet · Chorus of complaints · Cut and run · On an even keel · Photo finish

## Rhetorical question

A question to which no answer is expected, or to which only one answer can be made.

"The assumption is that only one answer is possible," says Fowler, "and that if the hearer is compelled to make it mentally himself it will impress him more than the speaker's statement. So *Who does not know . . . ?* for *Everyone knows,* and *Was ever such nonsense written?* for *Never was,* etc."

I missed the next name called, and had to ask the imp who the crane was that came faltering past in so undignified a fashion, with his head bent down so low that he looked back through his legs. "METATHESIS," said the imp. The crane maintained this odd posture even while the Queen was decorating him, so that she had to hang the medal over his tail. In response he sang:

> The head I once held very high
>     I now hold very low;
> I often make these shifts, though why
>     I make them I don't know.
>
> Do you recall Old English *brid?*
>     I changed it into *bird;*
> And *aks* I changed to *ask,* and *thrid*
>     I altered into *third.*
>
> Though now my head's between my feet,
>     Be not discomfited
> If you a year from now I greet
>     With feet between my head.

## Metathesis  me TATH uh sis  (Gr. "transposing").
The transposition of letters, sounds, or syllables in speech or writing.

If you say "revelant" for *relevant,* or "lobavle" for *lovable,* you are metathesizing. Words gradually change their spelling and pronunciation through metathesis. *Wasp* was once *waeps; clasp, clapse; fresh, ferse; thresh, therscan; hasp, haepse; thrill, thirle; curly, crulle.*

Metathesis in which the sound of a letter is transposed between two or more words is known as spoonerism, after the Reverend Dr. William A. Spooner, warden of New College, Oxford, whose notorious metatheses include these:

| | |
|---|---|
| "A well-boiled icicle" | for "A well-oiled bicycle" |
| "A blushing crow" | for "A crushing blow" |
| "Our shoving leopard" | for "Our loving shepherd" |
| "Our queer old dean" | for "Our dear old queen" |
| "Please sew me to another sheet" | for "Please show me to another seat" |
| "Someone is occupewing my pie" | for "Someone is occupying my pew" |
| "Kinkering congs" | for "Conquering kings" |
| "When the boys come home from France, we'll have the hags flung out" | for "When the boys come home from France, we'll have the flags hung out" |

**Stinky pinky**

A definition composed of an adjective and a noun that rhyme; a rhyming epithet.

| *The definition* | *The stinky pinky* |
|---|---|
| a mute elephant | Mumbo-Jumbo |
| criminal shellfish | mobster lobster |
| cattle rustler | beef thief |
| policeman's ball | cop hop |
| romantic young cat | smitten kitten |
| greased hen | slick chick |
| mouse in your kitchen wall | house mouse |
| one eager for aesthetic experience | culture vulture |
| umpire's baseball verdict | ball call |
| infested carpet | bug rug |
| blazing bed | hot cot |
| wagon for whores | tart cart |
| ardent employee | fervent servant |
| unimaginative surface decoration | prosaic mosaic |
| a cactus that goes out of its way to needle you | truculent succulent |
| a world of igneous rock | granite planet |
| boisterous policy meeting | raucous caucus |
| dismal chorus | dire choir |
| childish wall-painting | puerile mural |
| fanatic slave | zealot helot |
| fruitful interval of time | fecund second |
| New Yorker's wine cellar | Knickerbocker liquor locker |

—Philip Cohen, *Word Ways*

THE call "METONYMIA" evoked a glittering sword on legs. He flailed about as he walked to the platform, causing the creatures among whom he passed to draw back, and some of them to squeal. After accepting his decoration, he called to the audience, "Who am I?" They shouted back, "Warfare!" He turned into a crystal goblet, and called again, "Who am I?" This time they replied, "Strong drink!" When he had metamorphosed himself into several more such symbols, he became a sword again, and sang:

> Metonymy unloosed a wink,
>     And showed a Sword to stand for War.
> I don't know what he did this for,
>     Unless it was to make me think.
>
> He showed a Cup, and meant a Drink;
>     Showed Jezebel, and meant a Whore;
> I don't know what he did this for,
>     Unless it was to make me think.
>
> For Music he showed Humperdinck;
>     For Poetry his choice was More;
> For Thunderstorm he turned to Thor,
>     And called Confucius, meaning Chink.
>
> I don't know what he did this for,
>     Unless it was to make me think.

## Metonymia   me tahn i MEE uh   (Gr. "substitute meaning").
The evocation of an idea through a term for some substitute idea, or by putting cause for effect, or effect for cause.

In metonymia—metonymy to you and me—we read *the chair* for the officer sitting in the chair; *the press* for newspapers; *the scepter* for sovereignty; *Washington* for the federal government; *the bottle* for strong drink. *The crown* stands for the king or queen, *Shakespeare* for his plays, *a warm heart* for warm affections, *a good table* for good food. We say, "The pen is mightier than the sword," *pen* standing for what is written, and *sword* for military action.

> He is a man of the cloth.
> Blood is thicker than water.
> As learned commentators view / In Homer more than Homer knew. —Swift
> I should have been a pair of ragged claws / Scuttling across the floors of silent seas. —T. S. Eliot, "The Love Song of J. Alfred Prufrock"
> "Is the second floor at home?" "Somebody went out just now, but I think it was the attic which had been a-cleaning of himself." —Dickens, *Nicholas Nickleby*

ONOMATOPOEIA, a bird of red and orange plumage, with a long saber-shaped tail and a curved powerful bill, sang this:

> He thought I was a gay macaw
> (I mean by "gay" my color),
> With crimson tail and yellow claw,
> And breast but little duller.
>
> But when my utterance he heard,
> He knew I could not be a
> Macaw or any other bird:
> I'm Onomatopoeia.
>
> For kitten-like I mewed; I quacked
> Like ducks, and bayed like hounds;
> I dripped as faucets do—in fact
> Aped multitudes of sounds.
>
> 'Twixt click and honk and hiss and coo
> He never heard such racket,
> And then I laid an egg, and flew
> Off, crying, "Cut-ca-dacket."

She suited the actions to the words. The Gardener picked up the egg she had left behind, and settled it carefully in the Queen's flower basket.

## Onomatopoeia   ahn oh mat oh PEE uh   (Gr. "name-making").

The formation of words in imitation of natural sounds: *buzz, cuckoo, crack, hiss, bobwhite, babble, croak, puff-puff.*

Three theories of the origin of language, none now considered satisfactory, are called respectively: "bow-wow," "pooh-pooh," and "ding-dong." The "bow-wow" theory holds that words originated in imitations of natural sounds, such as those made by birds, dogs, and thunder; that is, the first words were onomatopoeiac. The "pooh-pooh" theory draws them from interjections—*uh! ow!* and the like. According to the "ding-dong" theory, sensory impressions triggered an associated sound in the human brain, as the stroke of a clapper causes a bell to ring. Each theory still has its backers, but it is unlikely that we shall ever know for sure how language began.

Some of the onomatopoeiac words listed by Peacham have disappeared long since: "Likewise we call a woman which delighteth much to hear tales and tell tales a flibergib, also trish-trash, tagnag or tagrag, hunch-lunch, riffraff, habnab, heave and hoe, clapperclaw, kickle-kackle."

### The word don't mean what you think it does
Many English words have foreign counterparts, identical in spelling but entirely different in meaning. Some examples:

> In Dutch, *aloud* means "very old"; *angel* means "sting"; *hark* means "rake"; *inner* means "collector"; *lover* means "foliage"; *room* means "cream"; *taken* means "jobs"; *wig* means "wedge."
>
> In Finnish, *alas* means "down"; *atlas* means "satin"; *into* means "enthusiasm"; *manner* means "mainland"; *pore* means "bubble"; *tie* means "road"; *vain* means "only"; *valve* means "awake."
>
> In French, *ail* means "garlic;" *ballot* means "bumpkin"; *enter* means "to graft"; *four* means "oven"; *lent* means "slow"; *lit* means "bed"; *mire* means "gun sight"; *teller* means "to send out roots."
>
> In Latin, *ago* means "I act"; *cur* means "why"; *dare* means "to give"; *fur* means "thief"; *limes* means "boundary"; *mane* means "early in the morning"; *probe* means "thoroughly"; *undo* means "wave."
>
> —Walter Penney, in *Word Ways*

If you were to give the English words listed above their foreign meanings, you would wind up with some odd sentences:

> I am aloud, he said; the room of life has soured; my takens are done. Men's taunts no longer angel, for the Great Inner is about to hark me in, and wig me into the earth beneath the green lover.
>
> (I am very old, he said; the cream of life has soured; my jobs are done. Men's taunts no longer sting, for the Great Collector is about to rake me in, and wedge me into the earth beneath the green foliage.)
>
> Without into I trudge alas the tie, hoping to remain valve until I reach the manner.
>
> (Without enthusiasm I trudge down the road, hoping to remain awake until I reach the mainland.)
>
> How long ago, and how probe, and even cur, depend on how mane the fur crosses my limes to eat my oranges.
>
> (How long I act, and how thoroughly, and even why, depend on how early in the morning the thief crosses my boundary to eat my oranges.)

OXYMORON was presented. His countenance caricatured the normal variance of shape between the right side and the left: his right side radiated good humor, while his left drooped in distress, as if his face combined the masks that represent Comedy and Tragedy. He sang as follows:

> I knew a mournful optimist
>> Of amply meager waist;
> With gentle cruelty he kissed,
>> And sluggardly made haste.
>
> Quick-slow was he, a tortoise-hare;
>> His eyes were keenly blind;
> His silence thundered in the air,
>> His face was on behind.
>
> A silly sage, a flowering weed,
>> Both slave and master he;
> Ah, bittersweet he was indeed,
>> My loving enemy!

## Oxymoron  ahk si MOR ahn  (Gr. "sharp-dull").
A figure in which an epithet of contrary meaning is added to a word.

An oxymoron, like a *paradox* (page 118), is often a mere contradiction in terms, but frequently makes perfect sense, as does Ralph Waldo Emerson's "Extremes meet, and there is no better example than the haughtiness of humility," or Thomas Hobbes's "Force and fraud are in war the two cardinal virtues."

His honor rooted in dishonor stood, / And faith unfaithful kept him falsely true. —Tennyson, *Lancelot and Elaine*
Their love was bittersweet.
That building is a little bit big and pretty ugly. —James Thurber

Wise folly · A cheerful pessimist · Harmonious discord · A deafening silence · With all deliberate speed

I had been confused enough by several of the creatures honored—Antithesis, for instance, who was his, her, or its own rhetorical mirror image; Litotes, who was this for want of being that; Oxymoron, who argued with himself. But none bewildered me so as PARADOXON, who now answered the Gardener's summons. Paradoxon was a color at once black and white, yet not gray; a tone at once bass and soprano, yet not midway between; a size at once large and small, yet not medium. Paradoxon was not a was, but he was a not. His appearance on the platform shifted by the second, yet my memory of him is clear: a figure in the appearance of a moon (a sun, rather), bowing before the Queen (kneeling, rather), and orating as follows (singing, rather):

> In artlessness I seek disguise;
> In ugliness my fairness lies;
> At hand am I when farthest off,
> And credulous when most I scoff;
> Most truthful when I lie, and most
> Unboasting when the most I boast.
> I find my happiness in tears,
> And grow my courage from my fears;
> On feebleness I build my strength,
> And measure brevity by length.
> When wisest, foolishest am I,
> And most shall live the day I die.

**Paradoxon**   pa ra DAHK sohn   (Gr. "incredible").
A statement that appears to contradict itself.

The force of seeming self-contradiction makes the paradox a forceful rhetorical device.

> As unknown, and yet well known; as dying, and, behold, we live; as chastened, and not killed; as sorrowful, yet always rejoicing; as poor, yet making many rich; as having nothing, and yet possessing all things. —2 Corinthians 6: 9–10
> Even throughout life, 'tis death that makes life life. —Browning, "The Ring and the Book"
> The swiftest traveler is he that goes afoot. —Thoreau, *Walden*
> We are for the most part more lonely when we go abroad among men than when we stay in our chambers. —Ibid.
> So wanton, light and false, my love, are you, / I am most faithless when I am most true. —Edna St. Vincent Millay, Sonnet X
> All was not lost until the moment when all had succeeded. —Napoleon after Waterloo

These paradoxical advertising headlines were collected by Don L. and Alleen P. Nilsen in *Language Play:*

The real beauty of it isn't the beauty of it—luggage
We're the same—only now we're better—a bank
What's it like to be a mother of three kids when you're already the father? —life insurance
A little compressor that is *very big*—engineering company

Other paradoxes:

The Detroit community is more than sixty percent minority. —Statement by a bank president in the *Detroit News*
In growing old, we become more foolish—and more wise. —La Rochefoucauld
The search for happiness is one of the chief sources of unhappiness. —Eric Hoffer
Asked whether he believed in free will or predestination, Isaac Bashevis Singer replied: "That's a very easy question. We have to believe in free will. We have no choice."
When you add to the truth, you subtract from it. —Yiddish saying

**Persiflage** PUR si flahzh (L. "whistle talk").
Light, bantering style in writing or speaking; idle, good-natured banter; raillery.

Persiflage is speech or writing with tongue in cheek. It combines irony, levity, and paradox, treating trifles as serious matters and serious matters as trifles.

Here is persiflage of pronunciation: If *ost* is pronounced as in "provost marshal," *lieut* as in the British version of "lieutenant," and *olon* as in "colonel," *nost lieut tolon* will be pronounced: "No left turn."

**P**ARANOMASIA was a circus clown; he turned cartwheels on his way to the stage, and blew soap bubbles while being decorated. His song was silly:

> *Extreme*'s a . . . dried-up riverbed,
> And *depth* is . . . height stood on its head;
> A *psychopath*'s a . . . crazy road;
> A *commentator*'s . . . just a spud;
> *Refuse* means . . . "put new fuses in,"
> And *Antiquate*'s . . . Aunt Katherine.
> *Ascent*'s a . . . rounded copper thing;
> *Relief* is . . . what trees do in spring;
> A *bluebird* . . . needs a chirp of cheer;
> *Arrears* are . . . organs used to hear.
> A *friar*'s a . . . religious hen;
> *Relent* is . . . money lent again;
> A *buttress* is a . . . female goat;
> A *horse doc* . . . has a croaking throat;
> A *crowbar*'s . . . where crows drink their toasts;
> A *boo-boo* is . . . a pair of ghosts.
> If owl and goat should make a match,
> The babe's a . . . *hootenanny,* natch.

**Paranomasia**   pa ra noh MAYZ ee uh   (Gr. "word-shunting"). Punning, playing on words, making jocular or suggestive use of similarity between different words or of a word's different senses.

Perhaps the most famous of puns is one that does not emerge in English translation: Jesus' statement to Peter "Thou art Peter [Greek *Petros*], and upon this rock [Greek *petra*] I will build my church."

"A good pun," say the Evanses in *A Dictionary of Contemporary American Usage,* "can be very witty. That is, under the incongruity there can be a suggestion of some deeper truth that usually goes unspoken; or that which is absurd by itself may have great wisdom, often bitter wisdom, when juxtaposed to the original statement. Puns were formerly used seriously, often to give a wry touch of bitterness or irony. Thus when the mad Lear says to the blinded Gloucester, *you see how this world goes,* Gloucester answers *I see it feelingly* and the word play heightens the horror. Mercutio's dying *Ask for me tomorrow and you shall find me a grave man* is in keeping with his character and its gaiety intensifies the tragedy of his death. With us, however, puns are now used solely for humor and hence they are excluded, by contemporary taste, from serious expression."

Familiar puns:

Tailor to man who brings in torn pants: "Euripides?"
   Man: "Yes; Eumenides?"
I am a tailor; my business is just sew-sew.
When I'm stoned, I get a little boulder.
When Jane spelled weather *w-e-t-h-i-r*, the teacher said,
   "That's the worst spell of weather we've had around here in years."

## Iconic Language
Communication through pictures rather than words.

I prophesied in *The Book of Predictions* (1981)—not quite seriously—that by 1992 all highway and direction signs will have turned into pictures. Many have done so already: A cigarette with a red line drawn through it means no smoking, a wriggling snakelike line means curves ahead, and so on. By 2030, I added, Chinese scholars will begin instructing American educators in the art of combining direction signs so as to convey complex ideas.

("this way") will merge with  ("that way") to make

meaning, "Can't you make up your mind?"

ERIPHRASIS was a sorrel horse, if a horse can have four pairs of legs, of which only the foremost and rearmost pairs function, the others hanging stunted and useless in between. He had also an extra tail, and an extra set of ears and eyes. He was not content to acknowledge his award with a single neighing song—he neighed two:

> When Per-i-*frays*-is* walks about, of legs he needs but four;
> To cut a finer figure, though, he grew as many more.
> His skill at biological redundancy applies
> To inner lights and livers, as to outer ears and eyes.
> He has so many extras in the way of lung and limb,
> He never can be sure himself which parts are really him.

> I summoned Per-i-*frays*-is,† and he came—
>    I say "he came," but not as others would;
> He first crawled east, but somehow missed his aim;
>    Next trotted north, which did as little good.

> He floated west, but could not find my trail;
>    He motored north, but did not see me there;
> He flew above the clouds, to no avail;
>    He burrowed deep . . . I wasn't anywhere.

> So roundabout and roundabout he spun,
> His wanderings were hard to understand.
> I'd thought his journey would be quickly done,
> Since all the while I held him by the hand.

**Periphrasis**   pe RIF ruh sis   (Gr. "expressing in a roundabout way").

The use of many words to express the sense of one; circumlocution.

Peacham: "When for *rhetoric,* we say *the art of speaking well;* for *logic, the art of reasoning;* for *tyrant, an oppressor of the laws and liberties of the commonweal;* for *man, a wight endowed with reason.*"

There was a time when periphrasis was accounted linguistic elegance. The fashionable writer said not *fish,* but "the finny tribe"; not *death,* but "the loss of life"; not *gun,* but "leveled tube." As late as the nineteenth century, Wordsworth was still referring to tea as "the fragrant beverage drawn from China's herb."

Periphrasis lends itself to unnatural construction of sentences, to passive terminology, and the like—that is, to jargon. The fashion today,

---

*He pronounced his name wrong so that the meter would be right.
†The pronunciation is *still* wrong.

though honored often in the breach, is toward the curt, concise, clear, compelling—the active rather than the passive, the Anglo-Saxon rather than the Latin. Yet periphrasis has its uses, and in the hands of an expert is not to be underestimated.

> I said the thing which was not. (I lied.) —Swift
> Now he is traveling the dark road to the place from which they say no one has ever returned. (He is dying.) —Catullus

WHEN I saw PLEONASMUS waddling past on his way to the platform, I said to my neighbor the red imp, "How can anyone be so fat? Or have such huge feet and hands?"

"He is not fat at all," said the imp. "It's the clothes he has on."

I looked again, and saw that Pleonasmus, who could scarcely have been four feet tall, was swaddled in layer on layer of trousers, shirts, sweaters, and jackets. He wore at least four pairs of shoes and as many of gloves, one pair over the other. On his head was a Stetson hat; on the Stetson, a derby; on the derby, a homburg; on the homburg, a deerstalker's cap; and on the cap, a panama. He had superimposed five pairs of spectacles over his eyes. As was to be expected, his footing was not good; he stumbled repeatedly, and once fell, lying on his back with his hands and legs waving in the air until a light bulb and a dustpan kindly helped him to his feet. When he had received his decoration, he bowed so low to the Queen that he fell again, but forward this time, so that he could push with his hands and feet and rise unaided.

He sang in a cheerful falsetto:

> With my own eyes an inn I spied;
> With my own feet I walked inside.
> With my own ears I heard you say,
> "You're not quite your own self today."
> With my own mind my meal I chose,
> And sniffed at it with my own nose.
> With my own mouth I ate my fill,
> And paid with my own dollar bill.

**Pleonasmus**   plee oh NAZ mus   (Gr. "abounding").
The use of words to state what is clear without them; sometimes used for emphasis.

> Let us gather together.
> Ears pierced while you wait.
> Twenty knots an hour.
> The reason why.
> Audible to my ear.
> The future lies ahead of us.
> I have seen no stranger sight since I was born.

Though pleonasms are commonly frowned on, they may be used with powerful effect:

> I saw a woman flayed the other day. And you would be surprised at the difference it made in her appearance for the worse. —Swift

THE red imp was good enough to let me use his opera glasses when PLOCE was on her way to the platform; for with my unaided eyes I could not quite make her out: she shimmered. The glasses brought her nearer and solidified her, so that I realized what had confused me: in right profile, she was a certain person; in three-quarters view, a different one; and in left profile, still another. It was as if an actress became in reality someone new in each new role she played. This was the rondolet she sang:

> Ploce glimmers, dark-in-light,
> Glooming here and glinting there.
> Ploce glimmers, dark-in-light:
> "Be not righteous, but be right";
> "Love loves lovers"; "Bear, forbear";
>
> "'Ware of him that cries 'Beware!' "
> Ploce glimmers, dark-in-light.

## Ploce   PLOHS ee   (Gr. "weaving; plaiting").
The repetition of a word with a new or specified sense, or with pregnant reference to its special significance.

> We want you to look good so that we will look good. —Advertisement for a cosmetic
> When the going gets tough, the tough get going.
> You were the life of my life.
> His wife is a wife indeed.
> Caesar was Caesar [that is, a merciful conqueror].
> Solomon was Solomon [that is, a man very wise].
> But islands of the blessed, bless you, son, / I never came upon a blessed one.
> —Robert Frost
> Dowered with the hate of hate, the scorn of scorn, / The love of love.
> —Tennyson, "The Poet"

A mountain reared above the stage, with sunlight flashing on its crest. Fleecy clouds encircled it, and silver glaciers lanced down its sides. I heard the queen say "PROSOPOPOEIA;" and where the mountain had been, an old man stood, bald on top, with white hair in a nimbus around his head and whiskers dropping from his chin in rapid spikes. When the queen had decorated him, he sang in a quavering falsetto:

> I treated Falsehood as a son;
> He turned to me his better side.
> Behold me, grieving and undone:
> No son was Falsehood—Falsehood lied.

And again:

> The robes of trees are green in spring;
> In autumn, many-hued.
> And here's a most contrary thing:
> In winter, trees go nude.

**Prosopopoeia**    proh soh poh PEE uh    (Gr. "the making of a person").
Personification of an idea.

Prosopopoeia was first the presentation of an absent person as if he were present and speaking; later it came to stand for personification, as when Dryden said: "These reasons are pathetically urged, and admirably raised by the prosopopoeia of nature speaking to her children." The tendency to attribute feelings, and hence personality, to inanimate things was called by John Ruskin the "pathetic fallacy." *Pathetic* here does not mean "exciting pity" but simply "having to do with emotion."

The woods leapt from their places, the ground did groan, the trees near at hand looked pale. —Ovid
[The stream] slumbers between broad prairies, kissing the long meadow grass, and bathes the overhanging boughs. —Hawthorne
Sing, O heavens; and be joyful, O earth; and break forth into singing, O mountains . . . —Isaiah 49:13.
These warm hills, rolling sensuous hills, full of milk. Some of them almost give a man an erection they are so voluptuously beautiful. —Sherwood Anderson
At length the dead cities, Troy, Mycenae, Argos, Ampipholis, Corinth, Sparta, will do a *danse macabre* with New York, Berlin, London, Paris. —Henry S. Haskins
Below, the coastline bares its teeth. —Alastair Reid, *Weatherings*
No time to turn at beauty's glance / And watch her feet, how they can dance. —W. H. Davies

## Abc language

A substitution of like-sounding letters, digits, or symbols for words or parts of words: "U R YY 4 me" (You are too wise for me).

ABC is a childhood pleasure which adults may enjoy also. It serves better for amusement than for communication.

### OIC

I'm in a 10der mood today
    & feel poetic 2;
4 fun I'll just — off a line
    & send it off 2 U.

I'm sorry you've been 6 O long;
    Don't B disconsol8;
But bear your ills with 42de,
    & they won't seem so gr8.
            —Unknown

ABC language is a kind of visual punning. In the following passage, translate O as either "O" or "cipher" or "sigh for" for sense:

U O a O but I O U;
O O no O but O O me;
O let not my O a O go,
But give O O I O U so.
            —William Whewell

**P**ROTROPE had an alligator's head, the body of a housefly, and the legs of an elephant. When his turn came, he stamped his thick feet, opened his tooth-lined jaws to their fullest, and sang:

> I swear you'll dine with me tonight . . . and let me tell you why:
> I have a tasty cheddar cheese, and salad that will do;
> There's trout caught fresh, and wine to suit, and homemade apple pie;
> There's coffee and there's brandy—and I owe a meal to you.

**Protrope**   proh TROHP ee   (Gr. "exhortation").
A promise to act, often with the reasons.

Traditionally, promises to act are most notable among lovers and politicians. The lovers generally make their promises in private, so they are not on record; but the promises of politicians are public, and can be turned against them. Protrope may also be *auxesis,* or *klimax:*

> France is invaded; I go to put myself at the head of my troops, and, with God's help and their valor, I hope soon to drive the enemy beyond the frontier. —Napoleon at Paris, 1814
> The allied powers having proclaimed that the Emperor Napoleon is the sole obstacle to the reestablishment of peace in Europe, he, faithful to his oath, declares that he is ready to descend from the throne, to quit France, and even to relinquish life, for the good of his country. —Napoleon's Act of Abdication, 1814

> I will not cease from mental fight,
> Nor shall my sword sleep in my hand
> Till we have built Jerusalem
> In England's green and pleasant land.
> —William Blake, *Milton*

I would have thought that SARCASMUS was Irony back again, for he had the same way of walking in one direction to travel in the other, and presenting the back of his head to show his face. But where Irony was a good-humored sort, neutral at worst, Sarcasmus seemed in a perpetual rage; the words of the song he sang were light, but the sound was furious:

> Oh, you're a fine one, ain't you!
>   A pretty sort are you!
> I can't think why folks paint you
>   In such an ugly hue!
>
> *You*'d never rob that blind man—
>   *You*'d never hit and run!
> Not such a sweet and kind man,
>   Who only kills for fun!
>
> Just show me one man dearer,
>   Or more a thoroughbred!
> (Take care now—one step nearer,
>   And, brother, you are dead!)

**Sarcasmus**    sar KAZ mus    (Gr. "tearing flesh; gnashing teeth").
A remark opposite in literal meaning to what is intended, conveyed typically in a sharply mocking or contemptuous fashion.

"The essence of sarcasm," says Fowler, in *Modern English Usage,* "is the intention of giving pain by (ironical or other) bitter words."

> It would not do to suppose that Negroes were men, lest it should turn out
>   that Whites were not. —Montesquieu

> "The man was in such deep distress,"
> Said Tom, "that I could do no less
> Than give him good advice." Said Jim:
> "If less could have been done for him
> I know you well enough, my son,
> To know that's what you would have done." —Ambrose Bierce

> ### Predestination
> We are the precious chosen few:
> Let all the rest be damned.
> There's only room for one or two;
> We can't have heaven crammed. —Unknown

> No picture of life in Calais was too ludicrous to be believed in Dover; that
>   is one of the advantages of being an island race. —Philip Guedalla, *Supers
>   and Supermen*

· 130 ·

I think I could be a good woman if I had five thousand a year. —Thackeray,
*Vanity Fair*

Things are going beautifully for me—as they do for saints in this world.
—Leo Rosten, *The Joys of Yiddish*

No egg on Friday Alph will eat,
  But drunken he will be
On Friday still. Oh, what a pure
  Religious man is he! —Anonymous

'Tis better to have loved and lost / Than never to have loved at all.
—Tennyson, *In Memoriam*

---

**Graffito**   (It. "a scratch")
A rudely scratched inscription, figure drawing, statement, etc.

A graffito frequently makes an unexpected point by a twist
on the language:

Help a nun kick her habit.
Support your local police station—steal.
The Lord giveth and the Lord taketh away.
(And underneath, in a different hand:)
Indian Giver be the name of the Lord.

The Nilsens (*Language Play*) collected these graffiti:

A home where the buffalo roam is messy.
Hit and run means never having to say you're sorry.
It is better to have loved and lost—much better.
If you've got half a mind to watch TV, that is enough.

WHEN Similitudo was called, I thought back to Metaphora, knowing there was a connection between them. Metaphora had been an owl; the images in his eyes had changed each time he blinked. But the connection escaped me, for Similitudo was a salamander, and though his color changed from red to purple to blue to green to yellow as he accepted his award, a salamander he unmistakably remained. This was his song:

> Upon a rock sits Simile, to sing
>     A song about herself, while echoes fly
> From skylark, linnet, robin on the wing.
>
> "'Tis I she sings of," sounds each avian cry;
> Then sun and moon and star cry, "No, 'tis I";
>     And sea and land cry, "No, she sings of me";
> "She sings of me," a cloud calls, drifting by;
>     And yet her song is but of Simile.
>
> Bird, sun, moon, star, sea, land, cloud—none deny
>     All these are in her song—all things that be;
>     And yet her song is but of Simile.

## Similitudo   si mil i TŌŌD oh   (L. "similar").

The comparison of two unlike things, made explicit typically by the use of the introductory *like* or *as*.

Fowler (*Modern English Usage*) lists three differences between a simile and a metaphor:

1. A simile is a comparison proclaimed as such, whereas a metaphor is a tacit comparison made by the substitution of the compared notion for the one to be illustrated.

2. The simile is usually worked out to some length and often includes many points of resemblance, whereas a metaphor is as often as not expressed in a single word.

3. In nine out of ten metaphors, the purpose is the practical one of presenting the notion in the most intelligible or convincing or arresting way, but nine out of ten similes are to be classed not as means of explanation or persuasion, but as ends in themselves, things of real or supposed beauty for which a suitable place is to be found.

Every simile is not a metaphor, and vice versa; but every metaphor presupposes a simile, and every simile is convertible into a metaphor.

> Errors, like straws, upon the surface flow.
> Reason is to faith as the eye to the telescope.

He keeps himself in the public eye like a cinder.

Lucentio slipped me, like his greyhound, / Which runs himself, and catches for his master. —Shakespeare, *The Taming of the Shrew*

Through all the weariness and disintegration their trained smiles flicked alight like a cuckoo clock striking in a bomb-smashed house. —Peter Dickinson, *The Lively Dead*

From morn
To noon he fell, from noon to dewy eve,
A summer's day; and with the setting sun
Dropp'd from the Zenith, like a falling star. —Milton, *Paradise Lost*

And the final event to himself [Burke] has been that, as he rose like a rocket, he fell like a stick —Thomas Paine, *Letter to the Addressers*

---

**Hendiadys**  hen DĪ uh dis  (Gr. "one by means of two").
The expression of an idea by two words connected by *and,* when normal usage would be to subordinate one to the other.

Hendiadys was a frequent ornament of Greek and Latin poetry, as in "Cupid shot an arrow and gold" for "Cupid shot a golden arrow." In English the usage is confined to a few informal expressions, such as "Just try and hit me" for "Just try to hit me," or "nice and cool" for "nicely cool."

> There will be ample opportunities . . . to try and insure the existence of a friendly Lebanese government. —*Wall Street Journal,* June 18, 1982

**S**YLLEPSIS!" called the Gardener. Atop the hill there appeared a circus rider, a black man dressed in black, standing on two snow-white horses, a foot on the spine of each. As he started his descent, another rider appeared beside him—a white man all in white, standing on two horses as black as coal.

"You cannot both be Syllepsis," cried the Gardener. "One of you is ZEUGMA! Zeugma, wait your turn!"

"Tell us which is which!" they demanded in chorus.

"Never mind," said the Queen. "Approach me together. I have decorations for you both." And when they arrived, she spread her butterfly wings and rose above the platform, hovering, as she hung their ribbons around their necks. Syllepsis and Zeugma brought their steeds about smartly so as to face us, and sang:

> Oh, Zeugma's dear, Syllepsis too,
>     and each to t'other twin;
> And with the both of them, my sweets,
>     it's love, it's love I'm in.
> To Zeugma but an hour ago I offered up my heart—
> Or else it was Syllepsis, for I can't tell them apart.
> How can I find solace in a lovely lover's spat
> Unless I have a way to know which one I'm angry at?
> "You lost your coat and temper," says Syllepsis of our tiff.
> "You left in fury and a Ford," says Zeugma. What's the diff?

**Syllepsis**   si LEP sis   (Gr. "a taking together").
A construction in which one word seems to be in the same relation to two or more other words, but in fact is not.

**Zeugma**   Z$\overline{OO}$G muh   (Gr. "a yoking").
The use of a word to modify or govern two or more words although its use is grammatically or logically correct with only one.

A syllepsis is grammatically correct, but requires that the single word be understandable in a different sense with each of its pair.

A zeugma uses the wrong word, and the appropriate word has to be supplied.

Syllepsis:

In his lectures, he leaned heavily on his desk and stale jokes.
She was seen washing her clothes with happiness and Pear's soap. (The first *with* means accompaniment, the second (implied) *with* means instrumentality.)

He lost his coat and his temper.

The new Oriental rug occupied most of the room and the conversation.
—Saki

Mr. Reagan clings to the economic theory that lowering taxes is enough to raise the tide and all the boats. But now the tide is out—and so is the truth. —Editorial, *New York Times*

"I am sorry to interrupt," he said in Italian and high dudgeon. —Robert Ludlum, *The Bourne Identity*

A zeugma:

See Pan with flocks, with fruits Pomona crowned. (Pomona is indeed crowned with fruits, but Pan is not crowned with flocks.)

"Although commonly a fault," says Fowler, "zeugma may, once in a great while, be used intentionally by a skillful writer." And he cites Pope's comment on Hampton Court:

> Here thou, great ANNA! whom three realms obey,
> Dost sometimes counsel take—and sometimes tea.

"The last line," Fowler declares, "is no blunder but one of the felicities of English poetry, not only because of the perfection of its humorous skill, but because of its touching suggestion that Queen Anne herself was a living zeugma, two unequal things yoked together: by the Grace of God, Defender of the Faith, Queen of England, Ireland, and Scotland, and, at the same time, a pathetic, dumpy, dull, lonely, little woman, sad with her dead babies, bored with her stupid husband, and far more at home at the tea than at the council table."

The 1981 election proved a lot less than it cost. —Editorial, *New York Times*

The Duke of Sussex said that the execution of the Russian band was perfect, which I denied, as their hanging was omitted. —Unknown

Chopin is entrammeled in the enthralling bonds of that arch-enchantress, George Sand, celebrated equally for the number and excellence of her romantic novels and her lovers. —*Musical World*, 1841

These are the citations—but I still cannot tell a syllepsis from a zeugma.

THE Gardener called another cat, this one named SYNATHROES-MUS. It was a very special sort of cat: a puss, pussy, pussycat; a kitten, kitty, kitty-cat; a tomcat, tom mouser, Chessy cat, silver cat, Chinchilla cat, blue cat, Maltese cat, tiger cat, tabby cat, tortoiseshell cat, calico cat, alley cat—part of all of these, or all of part of them. This was the song of Synathroesmus:

> O mangy cat, O scruffy cat,
> O one-eyed, bobtailed, toughy cat—
> You're fleas and meows from foot to head,
> You mouse-destructive quadruped!
>
> At times you are a lazy sort,
> A dozing, lackadaisy sort,
> A sleep-all-day-upon-the-bed-
> With-paws-upended quadruped;
>
> A give-the-sofa-leg-a-swipe,
> Rub-up-against-the-pantleg type:
> But still, dear cat, when all is said,
> A worth-the-bother quadruped.

## Synathroesmus   si na TREES mus   (Gr. "collection").
The piling up of adjectives.

Invective seems to lend itself more readily to the piling up of adjectives than praise does, and most of the tirades listed under *bdelygmia* would serve for synathroesmus as well. That is true for both of these:

He's a proud, haughty, consequential, turned-up-nosed peacock. —Dickens,
   *Nicholas Nickleby*
Of all the *bete*, clumsy, blundering, boggling, baboon-blooded stuff I ever
   saw on the human stage, that thing last night beat—as far as the story and
   acting went—and of all the affected, sapless, soulless, beginningless, end-
   less, topless, bottomless, topsyturviest, tuneless, scrannelpipiest—tongs
   and boniest—doggerel of sounds I ever endured the deadliness of, that
   eternity of nothing was the deadliest, as far as its sound went. —John
   Ruskin

**S**YNECDOCHE!" called the Gardener. At his summons, a smile appeared above the platform, with no face or body attached. Why, I thought, it is Alice's Cheshire cat! Still another cat! And I seemed to recall that this creature was identifiable by any of its detached parts, or several combined—eyes, mouth, whiskers, paws. Its nature was such that the entire cat might stroll by, yet nothing but its tail register in the observer's mind. How, I asked myself, could the Queen decorate an invisible cat? But her eyesight was evidently keener than mine; she hung the purple ribbon around the smile, and it remained there, with the medal suspended from it. The smile turned to an **O**, and Synecdoche announced, "I will now substitute the part for the whole." The smile then sang:

> "All hands on deck!" the captain cried;
>    But he was wroth to find
> That when the hands arrived on deck
>    They left the men behind.

"And now," announced Synecdoche, "the whole for the part:"

> "The law is upon us," cried safecracking Lardner,
>    "For poundin' I hear at the door!"
> "The law it is not, lad," responded his pardner.
>    "'Tis only Patrolman O'More."

And for an encore he sang:

> You say he reeled with *wine* in hand.
>    Not so; for truth to tell, he
> Had only emptied *glass* in hand;
>    The wine was in his belly.

**Synecdoche**   si NEK doh kee   (Gr. "receiving jointly").
The substitution of a more inclusive for a less inclusive term to describe something, or the other way around, as *mortal* for *man* (all men, but all other living things too, being mortal); or *sail* for *ship* (all ships formerly being equipped with sails).

Synecdoche is a form of *metonymia* (page 113), the evocation of one idea by associating it with another. Synecdoche narrows this to the association of a whole with one of its parts, or one part with the whole. A regiment of *foot* represents a regiment of *foot soldiers;* "Italy won the soccer match" means that the *Italian soccer team* won it.

Somebody stole his wheel. (His bicycle, of which the wheel is a part.)

The way to a man's heart is through his stomach. (*Heart* sums up the affections, and *stomach* the fleshly appetites.)

You must read me a little more slowly. Read all the words and laugh at all the jokes. —V. S. Naipaul ("Me" means "my written works.")

Wherever wood can swim, there I am sure to find this flag of England. —Napoleon (Ships in Napoleon's time were made of wood.)

Football kicker Lou Groza was called "the Toe," the outspoken baseball player and coach Leo Durocher was called "the Lip," actress Betty Grable was called "the Million-dollar Legs," and actor Jimmy Durante was called "the Schnoz." —Nilsen and Nilsen, *Language Play*

## Oddities from *Word Ways*

*Suoidea,* the name of the superfamily of pigs and peccaries, is the shortest English word in which the five vowels *(a, e, i, o, u)* occur in reverse order.

There are five accents in French *hétérogénéité.* Can you name a word that has more?

Ralph G. Beaman says the thirteen-letter word *breakthroughs* is the longest English word pronounced in only two syllables.

An Alaskan gazetteer lists *Qawiqsaqq,* a word with four *q's,* as the alternative spelling of Kawiksak, a bluff in Alaska.

Two flowers listed in Webster's Third have five hyphens each: *John-go-to-bed-at-noon* and *kiss-me-over-the-garden-gate.*

In Japanese promotion campaigns, the Scotch Tape slogan "Sticks like crazy" is said to have come out "Sticks foolishly," while "Body by Fisher" was rendered "Corpse by Fisher."

**T**HRENOS was a sprinkling can on legs. After the Queen hung his ribbon over his spout, he leaned forward, so that water squirted from him like tears, and sang:

> I was a babe. Ah me!—how sad to be
>     A babe! And then I turned into a boy—
> How sad to be a boy! And then a youth—ah me!—
>     To be a youth—how sad! And what annoy
> To grow up to a man! How sad! What tragedy!
>     Ah me, how sad, how sad! The years destroy:
> The hairs are falling from my head. I see
>     It's time to die. Ah me—to end all joy!—
> How sad! How sad! Let tears fall free, fall free!
>     Ah me—how sad, how sad!

**Threnos**  TRAYN ohs  (Gr. "dirge").
A lamentation, generally for the dead.

> Here a pretty baby lies
> Sung asleep with lullabies;
> Pray be silent, and not stir
> The easy earth that covers her.
> > —Robert Herrick

> Exult O shores, and ring O bells!
> But I with mournful tread
> Walk the deck my Captain lies,
> Fallen cold and dead.
> —Walt Whitman, "O Captain! My Captain!"

> She lived unknown, and few could know
> When Lucy ceased to be;
> But she is in her grave, and, oh,
> The difference to me!
> > —William Wordsworth, *Lucy*

**Epanorthosis**  e pan or THOHS is  (Gr. "a setting straight").
A correction of what one has uttered, generally to strengthen the point.

> He in a few minutes ravished this fair creature, or at least would have ravished her if she had not, by a timely compliance, prevented him. —Henry Fielding

There was such speed in her little body,
And such lightness in her footfall,
It is no wonder that her brown study
Astonishes us all.
     —John Crowe Ransom, "Bells for
        John Whiteside's Daughter"

But oh the heavy change, now thou art gone,
Now thou art gone and never must return!
     —Milton, *Lycidas*

TMESIS was a giant caterpillar of the kind called "woolly"; straight stiff hair, divided into bands of different colors, stood out from his body. The hair segments were separated by rings of nickel-colored metal, so that Tmesis appeared to be divided into several independent parts. This was what he sang:

> Tmesis (returning from some bloody where)
> Remarked, "It is abso-damn-lutely unfair,
> It's out-by-jing-rageous, it's in-by-jing-sane,
> Dis-horrible-gusting, for folks to maintain
> I must have grown up, from the twist of my talk,
> In Man-by-God-hattan in New-by-God-Yawk."

## Tmesis   TMEES is, MEES is   (Gr. "cutting").

The division of a compound word by the insertion of one or more words between its parts.

It is no longer usual in serious literature to slip an intervening word between the two parts of a compound, as Milton did when he wrote: "Which may soever man refer it." Tmesis continues in use, but generally for humorous effect. (Some grammarians compare a split infinitive to a tmesis, presumably because the infinitive in Latin was always a single word.)

Many examples of tmesis are run-of-the-mill: "where I go ever" for "wherever I go"; "what thing soever" for "whatsoever thing"; "to us-ward" for "toward us"; "chit and chat" for "chitchat." Frederic Packard, however, turned the form into art for *The New Yorker.* His tmeses, which he named "schizoverbia," were called to my attention nearly forty years later by Middy Darrow, and I list a sampling of them here, chuckling:

> "Oh, shut up, you ragged little muffins!" he yelled.
> "That fussy old budget."
> "Blathering bunch of skites."
> His income-tax return, he remarked, was the "most rigged-up marole" he'd ever seen.
> A friend who had acquired a major job was "going in for the highest damn faluting you could imagine."
> He described a group of men who came to a dinner wearing moth-eaten cutaways and striped trousers: "Never saw such a tattered bunch of dema-lions."
> Returning from a Christmas spent with a large family, including children of all ages: "The most jammed-up boree I ever went to, and a houseful of chattering little boxes."

T HE applause for Tmesis had scarcely faded when a horrid scream sounded from the top of the hill. We all looked up, to see a teacup and a saucer stagger through the gate, each holding to the other for support. What a pitiful spectacle they made! Both were smeared with tea stains. The saucer was chipped in half a dozen places, and cracked from edge to center. The cup was not only cracked, but its handle was gone; there must still have been a soggy tea bag at its bottom, for tea dribbled out of its wounds.

"Save yourselves!" they called in unison. "The pests are at the gates! The Solecisms are coming! They are just behind us! Fly, Queen, fly!"

She stood with her chin up and her frail shoulders squared. "The Queen does not fly!" she said; and the Gardener cried after her in a great voice, "The Queen does not fly!"

Now more remnants of her army appeared at the top of the hill, bloody and tattered, all crying, "Save yourselves!" The creatures in the audience were milling about, babbling and uncertain. But I could hear the Queen cry again, "The Queen does not fly!"

And then I heard that awful scuttling, and the vanguard of the pests —aphids, slugs, and thrips—cascaded over the top of the hill. The creatures below them fled in panic toward the stage. Once more the Queen cried out: "We have not lost, my dear children. It is up to you now, good Gardener; it is time for the secret weapon!"

I saw the handles of the bellows head begin to open and close faster and faster, until the speed turned them into a blur. A wind issued from the snout—such a wind as I had run into earlier, rising to a gale, to a hurricane. It passed quite over the terrified audience, to hit the surging garden pests head-on.

The pests—and me. This time I was caught up with them; together we were raised into the air and tumbled backward. For a moment I saw them spinning all about me. Then they were gone, and I was alone, riding head over heels above the Garden. I could see it spread out below me, the trees bending eastward in the wind. Vertigo caught me; I squeezed my eyes tight shut; I felt myself falling. There was a bump.

I was back in the lounging chair on the deck of the Red Cottage— no more Dandy Lion I. The wind was blowing furiously, and across the way a door in Michael Carter's empty house was slamming.

I did not go across to investigate.

# HENRY PEACHAM'S
# *The Garden of Eloquence*

HE great wind raised by the Gardener was sufficient to blow me out of the Garden once and for all, but I have no way of knowing whether it was as effective in blowing back the invading Solecisms. In fact, I suspect the contrary, for two reasons. First, I found the Gardener's members no longer in the shed, but back in their usual positions at my fireplace—the bellows hanging from a nail driven into the cement between two bricks; the tongs and poker in their rack; and the section of firewood upended on the hearth. I infer that the Gardener himself has been forced to flee. Second, as I return to listening to broadcasts and skimming through newspapers and magazines, I am forced to conclude that abuse of language, rampant enough before, is, if anything, speeding up; the workers in the Garden, if not vanquished, are clearly in retreat.

During my stay in the Garden arena, fifty or sixty rhetorical devices received decorations, but many more were still waiting their turn when the Solecisms invaded. I have returned to Henry Peacham's book on rhetoric to identify them.

There follow, in the Reverend Peacham's own words, descriptions of the Gardener's assistants who still wait to be decorated by the Queen.

# A NOTE ON
# HENRY PEACHAM'S
## The Garden of Eloquence

In the sixteenth century, when the Reverend Henry Peacham codified and illustrated the rules of rhetoric, Latin and Greek were reliable as authorities, for they no longer changed. But English, entering its lusty adolescence, was altering from book to book, and almost from one word to the next. Mr. Peacham capitalized or lowercased, as far as I can see, at random. He punctuated the same way. Like the rest of his generation, he blithely spelled words half a dozen different ways within half a dozen pages.

(Consistently, however, he spelled such words as *honor* and *judgment* in what is considered the American fashion today; the present British versions—*honour, judgement*—are the deviations.)

The extracts that follow from *The Garden of Eloquence* modify Peacham slightly, so as not to bewilder the reader, and for lack of space drop many of his illustrative sentences. With the examples given previously, however, they include all his rhetorical devices save a few that in my judgment have little modern relevance.

Sometimes Mr. Peacham forgot that he had dealt with some term, and discussed it a second time. Asyndeton, Enumeratio, Epanalepsis, Polysyndeton, and Zeugma are all described more than once. I have dropped the second references.

The author's favorite sources, Cicero and the Bible, unhappily are less familiar to twentieth-century readers than they were to Mr. Peacham's contemporaries. You may puzzle over what it was that Cicero had against Catiline, and who those Judges were to whom he appealed so constantly. It would make me very happy if you became intrigued enough to look up all these larger-than-life characters in your encyclopedia, even if it turns out that they really were not larger than life after all.

Since Mr. Peacham was a parson, it is not surprising that he turned *The Garden of Eloquence* into a moral tract. You cannot be expected to agree with all his interpretations of morality, though if you did it might do you good. But you are bound to delight in such revealing asides as: "Is it not a shame for thee, being an Englishman born, to despise the feat of shooting?" And again: "To be born and bred in Middlesex, and to speak ill English, is a foul fault."

If that is not Eloquence, dear reader, you will have to tell me what is.

# FIGURES

A Figure is a fashion of words, Oration, or sentence, made new by Art, turning from the common manner and custom of speaking. Figures are called of the Grecians Tropes and Schemates.

A Trope is an alteration of a word or sentence from the proper and natural signification to another not proper, but yet nigh and likely. Tropes of words are these: Metaphora, Metonomia, Synecdoche, Antonomasia, Onomatopoeia, Catachresis, Metalepsis, Antiphrasis, Acyrologia.

A Scheme is a fashion of writing or speaking made new by some art, and removed from the common custom. The difference between the Trope and the Scheme is this, that in the Trope there is a change of signification, but not in the Scheme.

**Adhortatio**    ad hor TAHT ee oh    (L. "encouraging; urging on").

Adhortatio, when we do exhort our hearers to do that which is profitable for them, after this manner. Virgil: Now now (quoth he), you Hector's mates, now cheerily stir your oars. Cicero: Wherefore you Judges look to yourselves, provide for your country, defend yourselves, your wives, your children and goods; maintain the renown and safety of the Roman people.

**Aenigma**   ee NIG muh   (Gr. "speaking in riddles").

Aenigma, a sentence of which for the darkness, there can be no certainty gathered. This Trope is more agreeable to Poets than to Orators, for every enigmatical sentence is obscure, and every Orator doth in speaking fly obscurity and dark speeches. *I consume my Mother that bare me, and eat up my Nurse that fed me, and then die, leaving them blind that saw me,* meant of the flame of a Candle, which when it hath consumed both match and tallow, goeth out, and leaveth them dark that saw by it. Another, *My mother begot me, and anon she is begotten of me again,* meant of Ice, frozen of Water, and resolved into water again.

**Aetiologia**   ee ti AHL oh jee uh   (Gr. "giving cause").

Aetiologia, when we join a clause to a proposition uttered. Amos 1: Thus sayeth the Lord, for three & four wickednesses of Tyrus, I will not spare him; because he did pursue his brother with the sword, and his anger did tear perpetually, and he kept his wrath forever.

**Alleotheta**   a lee OH thi tah   (Gr. "other placing").

Alleotheta, when we put one case for another, one gender for another, number for number, mood for mood, tense for tense, and person for person, whose kinds be these: Antiptotis, Enallage, Hendiadys, and Anthimeria.

**Anacoenosis**   a na see NOH sis   (Gr. "communication").

Anacoenosis, when either we ask our adversaries some counsel, or deliberate with the Judges, what is to be done, or ought to have been done. Thus, Paul to the Galatians: This only would I learn of you: received ye the spirit by the works of the Law? or by hearing of faith preached?

**Jargon**  JAR gun  (Old French "twittering").
Specialized or technical language; meaningless utterance; gibber-
ish.

   This is Mary J. Youngquist's jargonized version of the nursery
rhyme "Three Blind Mice:"

> A triumvirate of murine rodents totally devoid of ophthalmic acuity
> was observed in a state of rapid locomotion in pursuit of an agricul-
> turalist's uxorial adjunct. Said adjunct then performed a triple cau-
> dectomy utilizing an acutely honed bladed instrument generally
> used for subdivision of edible tissue.

Jargon sacrifices sense for secrecy (as in underworld slang) or
for security (as in political statements that straddle the issue). This
is how it is done:

> The problem is how to optimize the institutionalization of the fore-
> casting procedures. —From a discussion of British census proce-
> dures
> Totally obsolete teaching methods based on imprinting concepts
> instead of growthful actualizing of potential have created the in-
> tellectual ghetto. If schools would stop labeling cooperation
> "cheating," and adopt newer methods of student interaction, we
> wouldn't keep churning out these competitive isolates.—From a
> magazine for teachers (I think this means: "Let the kids cheat.")

Here is how Howard Bergerson in *Word Ways* cold-bloodedly
turns the axiom "Rolling stones gather no moss" into jargon:

> While briophytic plants are typically encountered on substrata of
> earthly or mineral matter in concreted state, discrete substrata ele-
> ments occasionally display a roughly spherical configuration which,
> in the presence of suitable gravitational and other effects, lends itself
> to a combined translatory and rotational motion. One notices in such
> cases an absence of the otherwise typical accretion of briophyta.

**Anapodoton**   a na POH duh tahn   (Gr. "not returned").

Anapodoton, an Oration wanting one member, or when in a sentence there is some little clause left out, either in the beginning, middle, or end, as Cicero in the seventh book to Atticus: Which if he do refuse, he shall be defied; but if he do accept them . . . so leaving of the other part unsaid, which is, If he do accept, and obey Pompeius's commandments, he will send Ambassadors, and entreat of peace.

**Antanaclasis**   an ta NAK luh sis   (Gr. "a returning to the matter").

Antanaclasis, when we repeat one word that hath two significations, and one of them contrary or at the least unlike to the other, thus: In thy youth learn some craft, that in thy age thou mayest get thy living without craft. Care for those things that shall discharge you of all care.

**Anthimeria**   an thi MEER ee uh   (Gr. "one part for another").

Anthimeria, when we put one part of speech for another, thus: So was all his life, for, Such was all his life (an adverb for an adjective); He spoke very hot you all can tell, for, He spoke very hotly you all can tell (an adjective for an adverb).

**Antipophora**   an ti PAHF or uh   (Gr. "against the allegation").

Antipophora, when we grant an objection, bringing in another thing which maketh the same objection tolerable. Cicero: I grant there is in it great labors, and many perils; yet by painful travail and valiant adventures therein shall ensue immortal glory.

ANTIPOPHORA

**Antiptosis**   an TIP toh sis   (Gr. "exchange" + "falling case").

Antiptosis, when we put one case for another, called also Enallage. Thus, I give you this gift with hearty good will, for, I give this gift to you with hearty good will (the accusative for the dative); he is condemned for murder, for, he is condemned of murder (the dative or accusative for the genitive); I am mindful in your matters, for, I am mindful of your matters (the ablative for the genitive).

**Apodioxis**   a poh di AHK sis   (Gr. "driving away").

Apodioxis, when we reject the objections of adversaries as trifles, or scorn them as absurdities, to which it is hard to answer, either saying they pertain not to the purpose, or feigning them to be foolish with laughing at them, or else promise to answer them at some more fit time, and so shake them off, with bringing in other matters. Cicero for Milo: What, should Milo hate Clodius the flower of his glory? Here is much ado to small purpose.

**Apostrophe**   a PAHS troh fee   (Gr. "turning away").

Apostrophe, when we suddenly forsake the former frame of our speech and go to another. That is to say, when we have long spoken of some person or thing, we leave speaking of it, and speak unto it, which is no other thing than a sudden removing from the third person to the second. Also it is called Apostrophe when we turn away to bring in some History, or fable, or something that is come even now to our remembrance, making as though we had not provided it of purpose, but that it came in mind we know not how. So mayest thou say, when thou hast spoken of the world, and showed the miseries, calamities, & cares thereof: O world, what sweet things dost thou promise, and how bitter dost thou pay; thy mirth is soon turned to mourning, and thy songs to sorrow.

**Articulus**   ar TIK yoo lus   (L. "dividing into joints").

Articulus, when one word is set from another by cutting the Oration, thus: Thou wast forewarned, admonished, gently entreated, and earnestly prayed to avoid this evil; thou hast lost thy substance, thy name, thy Parents, thy friends, and God thy Creator. Jeremiah 5: I will make them to be a reproof, a common byword, a laughingstock, a shame, &c.

**Asteismus**   a stay IZ mus   (Gr. "refined and witty talk").

Asteismus, a witty telling, in civil manner, and polishing our speech with some merry conceit, apt to move laughter of a sudden, as Cicero by often repeating of See, see, made the whole company fall a laughing, and caused Fabricius to cast down his head and depart from the bench. Such a man, quoth one, will say nay and take it; nay, quoth another, he will take it and say nothing.

**Asyndeton**   a SIN duh tahn   (Gr. "without conjunctions").

Asyndeton, a figure which keeps the parts of our speech together without help of any conjunctions, thus: I loved him, I delivered him, I set my whole delight in him. I never did it, I never spake it, I never thought it. Matthew 10: Heal the sick, cleanse the Lepers, raise the dead, cast out Devils.

**Bomphiologia**   bahm fi oh LOHJ ee uh   (Gr. "booming, buzzing words").

Bomphiologia, when trifling matters be set out with pretentious words, or else of such as would feign have their cunning wits known by setting out toys and trifling matters with lofty praises and great Eloquence. Evermore when words be as unmeet for the matter as a chain of Gold for an Ape, and a silver saddle for a Sow, then may it be called Bomphiologia.

**Brachiepia**   bra ki EEP ee uh   (Gr. "short word; short speech").

Brachiepia, when the matter is briefly told with no more words than those that be necessary, or when the Orator by brevity cutteth off the expectation of the hearer: As he passed by he took Lemnum, then he left a Garrison at Tarsus, after that he got a City in Bithynia, straightway won Abidus, &c.

**Cacemphaton**   ka SEM fuh tahn   (Gr. "ill-sounding").

Cacemphaton, when there come many syllables of one sound together in one sentence, like a continual jarring upon one String, thus: Neither honor nor nobility could move a naughty niggardly noddy; your strength is not to strive, or strike against the stream so strong; a planted place of pleasures plain, where pleasure shall me please; in my drowsy dreadful dream, I thought I drank of Dragons' deadly drink. Cacemphaton is of syllables, and Alliteration of first letters only.

**Cacosyntheton**   ka koh SIN the tahn   (Gr. "incorrect connection; bad placement").

Cacosyntheton, when good words be ill applied or placed, called a deformed composition, much like to Cacozelon, when good words be ill applied, thus: There is (quoth one) small *adversity* between your Mare and mine, for *diversity*. *

**Cacozelon**   ka KAHZ uh lahn   (Gr. "unhappy imitation or rivalry").

Cacozelon, an ill imitation or affection; that is, when words be used overthwartly, or contrarily for want of judgment; used of foolish folk who, coveting to tell an eloquent tale, do deface that which they would fain beautify; men not content to speak plain English, do desire to use words borrowed of the Latin tongue, imitating learned men, when they know no more their signification than a Goose; and therefore many times they apply them so contrarily, that wise men are enforced to laugh at their folly and absurdity: sometimes they will compound a word when it should be single, thus, it is an unthankless office, for thankless, or unthankful.

*Cacosyntheton today is known as malapropism.

**Malapropism**   MAL a prop izm
A grotesque and unintentional misuse of one word for another of
similar sound: *pretend* for *portend, fortuitously* for *fortunately*. (The
Greek word for this is *cacosyntheton,* "an incorrect connection.")

Malapropisms are named for Mrs. Malaprop, who in Sheri-
dan's comedy *The Rivals* was prone to such verbal blunders as "As
headstrong as an allegory on the banks of the Nile." In *Tom Brown
at Oxford,* Thomas Hughes raises the lowly malapropism to the
level of art:

> "Wut's to hinder thaay tryin' ov 'un, if thaay be minded to't?
> That's wut I wants to know."
> " 'Tis wut the counsellors call the Statut' o' Lamentations."
> "Wutever's Lamentations got to do wi't?"
> "A gurt deal, I tell 'ee. What do's thou know o' Lamentations?"
> "Lamentations cums afore Ezekiel in the Bible."

In *Fractured English,* Norton Mockridge collected hundreds of
malapropisms, including these:

She barbecues spareribs in her brassiere in the backyard.
A policeman drove a taxi in his off hours. He was moonshining.
The admiral was graduated from Indianapolis.
An appendix is something in the back of a book. If it gets in people
   it has to be taken out.
You could have knocked me over with a fender.
He wants his cake, but he doesn't want to eat it.
Frankly, I think he's barking up his sleeve.

**Charientismus**   ka ri ENT iz mus   (Gr. "expression of a disagreeable thing agreeably").

Charientismus, when we mitigate hard things with pleasant words, or thus, when with easy words matters very hard are mollified, as to say, Alas blame him not, youth will play such pranks now and then; let us forget trifles, and esteem weighty matters.

**Commendatio**   kah men DAHT ee oh   (L. "recommending").

Commendatio, when we highly commend some person or thing to our hearers, thus. Cicero: If Pompeius had been alive five hundred years ago, such a man he was, a young man and a Roman knight, the Senate might oftentimes have turned to him for aid and defense, whose noble acts and most renowned victories, both by land and Sea, had spread over all nations; whose three honorable triumphs are witnesses that all the world were in our governance and dominion; whom the people of Rome had commended with singular honors. Now if you should say that he did something against the league of peace, who would believe you? Truly no man, for when death had quenched envy, his noble acts would have flourished in glory of an eternal renown.

**Compar**   KAHM par   (L. "like").

Compar is when the members of an oration be almost of a just number of syllables, but yet the equality of the parts or members must not be measured upon our fingers, but be tried by a secret sense of the ear; for it is childish to tell the Syllables, when a few long do oftentimes match in measure many short; but exercise and practice may soon teach us to make the members accord very well and pleasantly. Proverbs 8: Through me do Princes bear rule, and all Judges of the Earth execute Judgment.

**Comparatio**   kahm pah RAHT ee oh   (L. "comparing").

Comparatio is a comparing of things, persons, deeds, examples, contraries, like or unlike. Cicero against Catiline: Truly if my servants should fear me as all thy Servants fear thee, I should be fain to forsake my house. Of the unlike: Marcellus restored to the Syracusans his enemies their Ornaments; Verres took away the same from his friends and companions. Sometimes a comparison is made with many degrees, whereof this shall be an example: If a man of his own good will should give thee a yearly stipend of twenty pound, ought you not to love him? And according to your power show yourself thankful for it? What ingratitude is it then, thus to neglect Christ, both God and Man, who besides bodily substance hath of his own good will given thee righteousness, who hath made thee partaker of his Heavenly gifts, who for thy sake fought with Satan, who wholly redeemed thee not with Money, but with his precious blood? Here the Oration groweth by many degrees from the less to the greater.

**Comprobatio**   kahm proh BAHT ee oh   (L. "approving wholly").

Comprobatio, when we see some good thing either in the Judges or in our hearers, or in any other. Cicero: I commend and praise you, you Judges, that most lovingly ye do advance the name of so famous a young man. Also, Believe me, you have done well in punishing so wicked a wretch, for now others may take example by him.

**Congeries**   KAHN jor eez   (L. "heap; pile").

Congeries, a multiplication or heaping together of many words, signifying divers things of like nature, thus. Paul to the Galatians 5: The deeds of the Flesh are manifest, which are these: adultery, fornication, uncleanness, wantonness, worshiping of Images, Witchcraft, hatred, zeal, wrath, strife, seditions, sects, envying, murder, Drunkenness, Gluttony, and such like. This figure forceth more by heaping than by increasing, and is nigh akin to Synonimia.

CONGLOBATIO

**Conglobatio**   kahn gloh BAHT ee oh   (L. "gathering into a ball").

Conglobatio, when we bring in many definitions of one thing, yet not such definitions as do declare the pith of the matter, but others of another kind all heaped together, which do amplify most pleasantly, such as be these definitions of Cicero in his second book of an Orator, by which he doth amplify the dignity of an History: an History, saith he, is a Testimony of times, a light of verity, the maintenance of memory, the Schoolmistress of life, the messenger of antiquity.

**Consolatio**   kahn soh LAHT ee oh   (L. "consoling; comforting").

Consolatio, when we seek means to take away conceived sorrow and heaviness from the minds of our hearers by comforting them with cheerful words, after this sort. Terence: Be of good cheer my sweetheart, hurt not thyself with sorrow, I warrant thee I will find out thy Pamphilus, wheresoever he be, & will bring him to thee.

**Correctio**   koh REKT ee oh   (L. "making straight").

Correctio, when we take away that that is said, and put a more meet thing in his place, whereof there be two kinds. The one is when a word is corrected before it be said, thus. Cicero: We have brought here before you, you Judges, to have your judgment, not a thief, but a violent robber; not an adulterer, but a breaker of all chastity; not a spoiler of church goods, but a rank enemy to all Godly religion; not a quarreling Ruffian, but a most cruel murderer.

Correction after the saying, thus. Now if he had but prayed his friends, nay had he done no more but beck, this might easily have been done, and that with small cost, nay with no cost at all; was he not a cruel wretch to do this? Nay, was he not a cruel beast to do such a wretched deed? He hath small shame, nay he is past all shame.

**Cronographia**   kroh noh GRAF ee uh   (Gr. "describing time").

Cronographia, when we do plainly describe any time for delectation's sake. Example. The Morning: When the bright beams of the East have driven away the dark shadow of the Night; when the Lark doth first mount on high, and welcometh the Morning shine with her cheerful song; when every living thing doth awake from sleep; when Birds fly from their night boughs abroad to seek their food; when Beasts arise from their night Lair, and fall to grazing; when men shake off their soft slumbers, rise up, and fall to labor.

**Diacope**   dī AK oh pee   (Gr. "a cutting in two").

Diacope, when a word is repeated, and but one word put between, thus. Thou knowest not (foolish man), thou knowest not what might and force virtue hath. Psalm 57: My heart is fixed, O God, my heart is fixed.

**Diaphora**   dī AF oh rah   (Gr. "distinction; difference; disagreement").

Diaphora, much like to Ploce, when the word repeated hath another signification; yet they differ, for Ploce repeateth a proper name, and this a common word, thus: What man is there living that would not have pitied that case if he had been a man? In the latter place man signifieth humanity, or the pitiful affection.

**Diasirmus**   dī AS uhr mus   (Gr. "disparagement; ridicule").

Diasirmus, when we delude the reasons of our adversaries, and so, by scoffing, debate their authority, as to say to one's opponent that he fights with lead Daggers, meaning weak and slender Arguments.

**Diastole**   dī AST oh lee   (Gr. "expanding").

Diastole, when a short Syllable is made long, necessity of meter so compelling, as PalEmon for Palemon, ArmenIa for Armenia, Commend-ABle for Commendable, OrphEus for Orpheus.

**Digresio**   di GRES ee oh   (L. "going aside").

Digresio is the handling of some matter out of order, yet for profit of some pertinent cause. We may digress for cause of praising, dispraising, delighting, or preparing. Now we must first see why we should digress, and that the digression may some manner of way profit the cause that we have in hand. Also we must have a perfect way provided beforehand that we may go forth aptly, and making no long tarriance out, return in again cunningly. We darken the matter if we break forth by violence, and bring in matters very strange and far off, or much unlike to the cause put forth; such digressions happen often to those that lack the knowledge of Rhetoric. This figure is a virtue whereby the Oration is garnished, beautified and commended; otherwise it is a vice that doth deform and patch the Oration with broken pieces.

**Dilemma**   di LEM uh   (Gr. "ambiguous proposition").

Dilemma, when we divide a thing into two parts, and reprove them both by showing reasons. Cicero: How did he slay him—without any help, or had he others at his commandment? If thou dost accuse him, he was not at Rome; if thou sayest he did it by others, I demand by what manner of men—by Servants, or by free men?

**Dinumeratio**   di nōō muh RAHT ee oh   (L. "reckoning up").

Dinumeratio, when we number up many things for love of amplifying. Paul to the Corinthians 11: Are they ministers of Christ? I am more; in labors more abundant, in stripes above measure, in prisons more frequent, in death oft. Of the Jews five times received I forty stripes save one. Thrice was I beaten with rods, once was I stoned, thrice I suffered shipwreck, a night and a day have I been in the deep. In journeyings often, in perils of waters, in perils of robbers, in perils by the heathen, in perils in the city, in perils in the wilderness, in perils in the sea, in perils among false brethren. In weariness and painfulness, in watchings often, in hunger and thirst, in fastings often, in cold and nakedness.

This differeth from Congeries, for Congeries heapeth up words, and this sentences.

**Dirimens copulatio**   DIR i mens kahp yōō LAHT ee oh   (L. "breaking the connection").

Dirimens copulatio, when we bring forth one sentence with an exception before it, and immediately join another after it that seemeth greater. Cicero, giving the Roman people thanks for his return: You have, saith he, not only taken away my calamity, but also seem to augment my dignity.

**Distributio**   dis tri BYŌŌT ee oh   (L. "dividing; distributing").

Distributio, when we dilate and spread abroad the general kind by numbering and reckoning up the special kinds; the whole by dividing it into parts; and the subjects by rehearsing the accidences.

**Divisio**   di VIZ ee oh   (L. "forcing asunder; cleaving").

Divisio, which removing one thing from another endeth them both by showing a reason. Cicero for Ligarius: I demand now whether you will revenge your own injuries, or the injuries of the commonwealth. If you do revenge the injury of the commonwealth, what answer will you make concerning your constancy in that behalf if you do revenge your own? Beware you err not, which think that Caesar will be angry, and have displeasure with your enemies, when he hath forgiven his own.

**Ecphonesis**    ek foh NEE sis    (Gr. "exclamation").

Ecphonesis, when through affection either of anger, sorrow, gladness, marvelling, fear, or any such like, we break out in voice with an exclamation & outcry to express the passions of our mind, after this manner: O lamentable estate; O cursed misery; O wicked impudency; O joy incomparable; O rare and singular beauty. Paul to the Romans 7: O wretched man that I am, who shall deliver me from this body, subdued unto Death.

**Emphasis**    EM fuh sis    (Gr. "exhibiting; indicating").

Emphasis, when there is more to be understood than the words by themselves do express; and it is after divers manner of ways used; sometimes by Hyperbole, as, My man is become a Lord of late; whereby is signified that the same servant is waxen proud and disobedient, setting light his master's commandment; sometimes in one word, as, Help now, you men that would me well; the Adverb now containeth an Emphasis, as much to say, if you do not help me now, I am utterly undone; help now or else never. By things going before, we signify things following after, as, Amend your life, Father, you are an old man: by putting him in mind that he is old, we signify that Death is next to old age, and after Death cometh Judgment, when it is too late to repent.

**Enallage**    e NAHL uh jee    (Gr. "changing").

*Of gender*

Enallage of Gender, when we put the Neuter for the Masculine or Feminine, or any one of them for another, thus: He doth bear a countenance as if it were an Emperor, for, as if he were an Emperor. The Neuter for the Masculine: It is a wicked daughter that despiseth her mother, because she is old, for, She is a wicked daughter, &c.

*Of number*

Enallage of Number, when the singular number is put for the plural, or the plural for the singular. Thus, Pliny on Africa: The greater part of wild beasts do not drink in summer for want of showers. Here the plural is put for the singular, for the greater part is the singular number, and therefore so should the verb be singular also.

ENTHIMEMA

### Of mood

Enallage of Mood, when we put the Indicative for the Imperative or Subjunctive, the Potential for the Indicative, or any of them one for another, thus: My loving friends, we will not break our promise made, for, Let us not break our promise made (the indicative for the imperative). I am sorry that I hear it, for I am sorry to hear it (the subjunctive for the infinitive).

### Of time

Enallage of Time, when we put one time for another, thus. Terence: I come to the maidens, I ask who she is, they say the sister of Christ, for, I came to the maidens, I asked who she was, they said the sister of Christ. The present tense for the preterperfect tense: If it happen hereafter that they may bear rule, we are all undone, for, shall be all undone.

### Of person

Enallage of Person, when one person is put for another, thus, Here he is, what have you to say unto him, speaking of himself, for, Here I am, what have you to say unto me.

## Enthimema    en thi MEEM uh    (Gr. "having in mind").

Enthimema is another kind of sentence which standeth of contraries, thus. Cicero: If wicked men so much commend you, good men must needs dispraise you; if great wealth bring carefulness, a needy poverty wretchedness, then the mean between those extremes is the greatest happiness.

## Enumeratio    e nōōm or AHT ee oh    (L. "counting out").

Enumeratio, when we gather together those things into a certain number, which straightway we do briefly declare. Ecclesiastes 25: Three things there are that my spirit favoreth, which be also allowed before God and man: the unity of brethren; the love of neighbors; a man and wife that agree well together. Three things there be which my soul hateth, and I utterly abhor the like of them: a poor man that is proud; a rich man that is a liar; and an old body that doteth, and is unchaste.

**Epanodos**   e PAN oh dahs   (Gr. "repetition of the same sound; dou-bling").

Epanodos, when we iterate by parts the whole spoken before, signify-ing a certain diversity in the parts which are divided, thus. Paul to the Corinthians 2: For we are unto God a sweet savor of Christ, in them that are saved, and in them that perish. To the one we are the savor of death unto death; and to the other the savor of life unto life.

**Palindromos**   pal in DROHM ohs   (Gr. "running back again"). A word, phrase, verse, or sentence that reads the same backward as forward: "Madam, I'm Adam."

As I mentioned in another book, the first known palindrome in English sprang in the seventeenth century from the antic mind of John Taylor, known as the "Water Poet" because it was on the Thames River that he sculled, collected revenues on wines from ships in passage, and once sailed briefly in a boat made of brown paper. Taylor's pioneering line ran: "Lewd I did live, & evil did I dwel."

"Dwel," though now an erroneous spelling, was fine in the Water Poet's time; but even with that advantage, he had to use an ampersand (&) for "and" to make the palindrome work. Nearly two hundred years passed before the next recorded English palin-drome—though there was at least one meantime in Welsh, "Liad ded dail," meaning "holy blind father."

In 1821, the former Emperor Napoleon died, an event cele-brated by an unremembered wit with the palindromic line "Able was I ere I saw Elba." Thereafter palindromes came fast. The *Monthly Magazine and Literary Journal,* which just before Napoleon's death had complained that English did not lend itself to the form, printed such specimens as:

**Epanalepsis**   e PAN uh LEP sis   (Gr. "taking up").

Epanalepsis, when that is repeated in the end of a sentence that was set in the beginning, the construction being perfect without such repetition, thus. Farewell my friends with bitter tears, a thousand times farewell. Virgil: Many things of Priam she did demand and of Hector many things.

---

A limner, by photography dead beat in his position,
Thus grumbled: *"No, it is opposed; art sees trade's opposition";*

A timid creature, fearing rodents, mice, and such small fry,
*"Stop, Syrian, I start at rats in airy spots"* might cry.

Among the elegant palindromes of the nineteenth century were: "I, man, am regal; a German am I"; "Sums are not set as a test on Erasmus"; the conscript's complaint "Snug & raw was I ere I saw war & guns"; and the gloomy "Egad, a base tone denotes a bad age." More recently, Howard W. Bergerson celebrated the building of the Panama Canal by Colonel G. W. Goethals with: "A man, a plan, a canal—Panama." Other familiar specimens are: "Step on no pets"; "Never odd or even"; and "Sex at noon taxes." Alastair Reid wrote: "T. Eliot, top bard, notes putrid tang emanating, is sad. I'd assign it a name: 'Gnat dirt upset on drab pot toilet.' " (This has been erroneously attributed to W. H. Auden.) "He goddam mad dog, eh?" is by James Thurber. I don't know who wrote "Now, Ned, I am a maiden nun; Ned, I am a maiden won." But I do know that in the 1980 presidential campaign, Edward Scher composed: "To last, Carter retracts a lot."

There are palindromes that contain as many as five thousand letters, but when longer than fifty or sixty they do not make much sense.

**Epanaphora**    e pa NAF oh rah    (Gr. "recurrence").

Epanaphora, when one word is repeated in the beginning of divers clauses, as thus, Cicero in the praise of Pompeius: A witness is Italy, which was by the virtue and counsel of this man delivered. A witness is Cilicia, which being environed on every side with many and great dangers, he set at liberty, not with terror of war, but quickness of counsel. A witness is Africa, which being oppressed with great armies of enemies, flowed with blood of slain men.

**Epexegesis**    e PEK suh jee sis    (Gr. "detailed narrative").

Epexegesis is an added interpretation, that is, when we interpret the words or sentence going before by another sentence coming after, in this manner. Paul to the Romans 2: When shall be opened the righteous judgment of God, which will reward every man according to his deeds; that is to say, Praise, honor, and immortality to them which continue in good doing and seek immortality; but unto them that are Rebels, and do not obey the truth, but follow unrighteousness, shall come indignation, wrath, tribulation, &c.

**Epiphonema**    e pi foh NEEM uh    (Gr. "speaking out").

Epiphonema, an acclamation of a matter uttered or approved, containing the sum and conclusion thereof. Virgil: So weighty a matter it was to set up the Roman nation, so hard a matter it is to call again the voluptuous man from vice, and the covetous man from his greedy desire. This figure is evermore used after the matter is told or approved, which maketh an end of the same, with much more marvelling; that is to say, an amplifying of honesty, wickedness, pleasure, dignity, profit, loss, difficulty, and such like.

**Anagram**   AN a gram   (Gr. "backward letters").
A word or phrase formed by reordering the letters of another word
or phrase, as: *opts, pots, tops, stop, post.*

   Members of the National Puzzlers League uncovered most of
the following anagrams:

| | |
|---|---|
| Credential | Interlaced |
| Lionesses | Noiseless |
| Ocean | Canoe |
| Prettiness | Persistent |
| Pictures | Piecrust |
| Sunlight | Hustling |
| Aphrodite | Atrophied |
| Impregnate | Permeating |

   A rearranged word or saying that comments on the sense of
the earlier letter arrangement is called an "elegant" anagram. For
instance:

| | |
|---|---|
| Tower of London | One old fort now |
| The U.S. Library of Congress | It's only for research bugs |
| The Beatles | These bleat |
| | —Darryl H. Francis, in *Word Ways* |

| | |
|---|---|
| The United States of America | Attaineth its cause—freedom |
| The eyes | They see |
| A sentence of death | Faces one at the end |
| | —Dmitri A. Borgmann |

| | |
|---|---|
| Atom bombs | A mob's tomb |
| | —Howard Bergerson |

| | |
|---|---|
| Archsaint | Anarchist |
| Lee, darling! A big icy diamond! | I'm only a bird in a gilded cage |

**Epiphora**  e PIF oh rah  (Gr. "a bringing to or upon").

Epiphora, when many members or clauses do end still with one and the same word (contrary to Epanaphora), thus: Since the time that concord was taken from the city, liberty was taken away, fidelity was taken away, friendship was taken away. Matthew: Have we not prophesied in thy name, have we not cast out devils in thy name, and done many miracles in thy name?

**Epitheton**  e PITH uh tahn  (Gr. "an addition").

Epitheton, when we join Adjectives to those Substantives to whom they do properly belong, and that either to praise, dispraise, to amplify, or extenuate. To praise, thus: Cicero for Ligarius, O wonderful clemency, also, O most holy Discipline, O glorious act, O noble renown, O heavenly joys. Contrariwise to dispraise: O filthy fornication, O wicked man, O insatiable desires, O most shameful face.

**Epitrope**  e PIT roh pee  (Gr. "reference; arbitration").

Epitrope is a kind of permission, when we grant anything ironically. Simo in Terence seemeth by his words to grant very willingly that his son might marry Glicery, when indeed he did with all diligence endeavor to withdraw his son from her; yes, quoth he, let him take her, God send him good speed, let him go dwell with her. So commonly when one part with a thing against his will, he will say, much good may it do you, I am glad with all my heart you have it, when his meaning (God wot) is clean contrary.

**Erotema**  e roh TEEM uh  (Gr. "question").

Erotema, when by demanding, we either affirm or deny something strongly. Cicero for Cluentius: Hath not Fidicularius declared the cause? for, Without doubt Fidicularius hath declared the cause. Job 22: Is not thy wickedness great, and thine ungracious deeds innumerable?

**Expeditio**   ek spe DIT ee oh   (L. "freeing the feet; extrication").

Expeditio, when many reasons being reckoned by which something may either be done or not done, one reason is left, which we stand unto and conclude upon, and the others are taken away, thus. Seeing this ground was mine, thou must needs show that either thou possessed it being empty, or made it thine by use, or bought it, or that it came unto thee by heritage. Thou couldst not possess it empty when I was present; thou canst not make it thine by use; thou hast not shown that thou boughtest it; it could not come to thee by heritage and I alive. It followeth then that thou wouldst put me from my own ground before I be dead.

**Expolitio**   eks poh LIT ee oh   (L. "polishing").

Expolitio, when we abide still in one place yet seem to speak many things, many times repeating one sentence, but with other words and figures. Of this figure there be three kinds. One is when we do vary one thing or sentence divers manner of ways, and entreat of it with sundry fashions of speech. This first kind is called Synonimia, whereof shall be said later. Secondly, by altering of pronunciation; that is, when the Orator doth occupy or repeat the same words & sentences with an alteration of his voice & gesture. Thirdly, by alteration of the handling, or entreating, as when the Orator conveyeth his speech either to Prosopopeia, or to Exuscitation. Cicero, having most grievously accused Catiline in the Senate, commandeth him to get him out of the City, but changeth the handling of his sentence, and translateth his speech to Prosopopeia, and rehearseth in order all his ungracious deeds against the City, accusing him sore, and willing him to depart out of it: There hath, sayeth he, no abominable deed been heard or seen these many years, but through thee; no naughty facts without thee.

**Exuscitatio**   ek sōō si TAHT ee oh   (L. "rousing up; wakening").

Exuscitatio, when the Orator showeth himself much moved by the utterance of his speech, and thereby likewise moveth the minds of his

GNOME

hearers, and it is used when persons or matters do require either great praises or dispraises. In praises, thus: What man is he, be he never so envious, never so malicious, never so ambitious of praise, but must needs commend this man, and acknowledge him to be most virtuous, most learned, most wise? In dispraises, thus: Who is of so careless a mind that seeing these things can hold their peace and let them pass? You put my father to death before he was condemned, & being put to death, you registered him among the number of condemned men; you thrust me out of mine own house by violence; you possessed my patrimony; what will you more?

**Frequentatio**    fray kwen TAHT ee oh    (L. "a crowd").
    Frequentatio, when matters dispersed throughout the whole are gathered together in one place, whereby the Oration is made more pithy and sharp, or thus: When all is done, what vice is he free from, what is the cause wherefor you Judges would deliver him? He is a betrayer of his own chastity, he lieth in wait for others, he is covetous, he is intemperate, vicious, proud, wicked to his parents, unkind to his friends, troublesome to his kinsmen, stubborn to his betters, disdainful to his fellows and equals, cruel to his inferiors, finally, intolerable to all men.

**Gnome**    NOHM, NOHM i    (Gr. "intelligence; maxim").
    Gnome, a saying pertaining to the manners and common practices of men, which declareth by an apt brevity what in this our life ought to be done or not done. Whereof there be sundry kinds. The first, a sentence universal, which containeth no certain person or thing, thus. Ill gotten goods are soon spent; envy is a punishment to himself. The second is a single sentence, as: A city in sedition cannot be safe; The contented man is very rich. The third is a double sentence, as: True glory taketh deep root and continueth long, but all counterfeit things do quickly fall away, and perish as the blossoms. The fourth, a sentence without showing a reason, as: It is the duty of a young man to reverence his elders. The fifth, a sentence with a reason, as: It is the part of a constant man to excel so much in virtue that he shall not need to fear the blame of Fortune. The

sixth is a sentence of contraries, as: After labor and diligence followeth wealth and riches; but after sloth and idleness cometh poverty and neediness. The seventh is a sentence of divers things, as: Death is not miserable, but the way and passage to death is miserable. The eighth is a sentence showing what doth hap in life, as: Things do alter daily, pride goeth before, and shame cometh after. The ninth is a pure sentence, not mixed with any figure, as: The covetous man wanteth as well that which he hath not. The tenth is a figured sentence whereof there be as many kinds as there be figures; and if it be figured, it hath the name of the same figure wherewith it is joined.

**Gratiarum actio**    gra ti AR uhm AK tee oh    (L. "thanks").

Gratiarum actio, when we give the Judges or our hearers most hearty thanks for the favor that we have obtained of them, and for their gentleness in granting to our desire or request, and sometimes also for their patience in hearing us. Cicero: To thee, O Caesar, we give most hearty thanks, yea, great thanks we yield to thee. John 11: Father I thank thee that thou hast heard me.

**Hendiadys**    hen DĪ uh dis    (Gr. "one by means of two").

Hendiadys, when a Substantive is put for an Adjective of the same signification, as when we say, He is a man of great wisdom, for, He is a very wise man; a saying of comfort, for, a comfortable saying; A man of great wealth, for, a wealthy man.

**Homoptoton**    hoh MAHPT oh tahn    (Gr. "falling; declining").

Homoptoton, when divers clauses do end alike by cases: He was to good men profitable; to his enemies terrible; in virtues most commendable; obtaining a name forever durable. Our desires are full of disquietness, and our doings are clogged with weariness. Ecclesiastes 22: Be faithful to thy neighbor in his poverty that thou mayest rejoice with him in his prosperity.

HENDIADYS

**Homotelenton**   hoh moh TEL en tahn   (Gr. "a like ending").

Homotelenton, like to Homoptoton, when divers clauses do end alike by Verbs or Adverbs, thus: Eloquent is he which can invent excellently, dispose evidently, figure diversely, remember perfectly, and pronounce magnifically. Another: Her beauty was commended, her Learning praised, her virtues extolled, and her worthy deeds well remembered.

**Horysmos**   hoh RIZ mus   (Gr. "marking out by boundaries, limitations").

Horysmos, when we declare briefly and perfectly the proper pith of something; and it is chiefly used when there is a difference sought for between two words, which by defining this findeth forth, thus: This is not Fortitude, but Temerity; for Fortitude is a contempt of perils by honest reason; Temerity is a rash and foolish enterprise of perils, without respect of Virtue. Again, this is not Diligence, but Covetousness; for diligence is a chary and careful keeping of those things which be his own, covetousness is an injurious desire of other men's goods.

**Hypallage**   hī PAHL uh jee   (Gr. "exchanging").

Hypallage, when a sentence is said with a contrary order of words, as, He took his ear from his fist; Open the day, and see if it be the window; I would make no more ado, but take a door and break open the Axe.

**Hyperbaton**   hī PUHR ba tahn   (Gr. "stepping over").

Hyperbaton, when the right and lawful order of words or clauses is altered by improper placing, or thus: when words or clauses be transposed from the plain order of construction, to make the oration more lofty. Cicero calleth it an apt and pretty bearing over of words. Virgil: What heart can of the Greeks or soldiers, Ulysses' route refrain to weep? This construction differs from Anastrophe, which is a preposterous rendering, while Hyperbaton adds force to the message.

**Hypophora**   hi PAHF oh ruh   (Gr. "objection").

Hypophora, when we answer to our own demand, thus: I demand how this man is now become so rich; had he any patrimony left him? No, all his father's goods were sold. Had he any inheritance? It cannot be said, for he was disinherited from all things necessary. The Author to Herennius: When our ancestors had condemned any woman of one offence, they supposed her by plain judgment to be convicted of many. By what reason? For whom they judged unchaste in living, they thought her also condemned of poisoning. Why so? Because it must needs be that she which doth addict her body to filthy lust, doth fear many. Who be they? Her husband, her parents, and others to whom she sees the infamy of her dishonesty doth obtain. What then? It must needs be that she would by some means gladly poison them whom she fears so much. Wherefor? Because there is no honest means to hold her back, whom the greatness of the fault maketh fearful, intemperancy bold, woman's nature quick.

**Hypotiposis**   hī poh TIP oh sis   (Gr. "sketch; outline").

Hypotiposis, like unto Icon, a description of persons, things, places, and times; and it is, when by a diligent gathering together of circumstances, we express & set forth a thing so plainly that it seemeth rather painted in tables than expressed with words, and the hearer shall rather think he see it than hear it. By this figure the Orator doth as it were point out each thing in his due color, for even as the cunning Painter painteth all manner of things most lively to the eyes of the beholder, bestowing his colors in their proper places, and framing Images of all forms and fashions, some smiling, some weeping, some with furious look, some as though they were busily occupied, some dead, some asleep, some old; finally all degrees in their countenance and apparel, even so doth the Orator by words set forth any person according to his age, stature, color, complexion, gesture, countenance, manners, and qualities, so that the hearer shall think he doth plainly behold him; and so likewise in any other thing.

### Tongue twister

A word or words difficult to articulate rapidly, usually because of a succession of similar consonantal sounds.

We are familiar with "How much wood would a woodchuck chuck if a woodchuck would chuck wood?" We know, too, that "Peter Piper picked a peck of pickled peppers." Some other passages that tangle the tongue:

> Whip gig, whip gig, whip gig, whip gig (etc.).
> Troy boat, troy boat, troy boat, troy boat (etc.).
> Bug's bad blood.
> The skunk sat on a stump; the skunk thunk the stump stunk, but the stump thunk the skunk stunk.
>
> If you stick a stock of liquor in your locker,
>     It is slick to stick a lock upon your stock,
> Or some joker who is slicker's going to trick you of
>     your liquor . . .
> If you fail to lock your liquor with a lock."
>
> —Newman Levy
>
> The curious cream-colored cat crept into the crypt, crapped, and crept out again.
> Show me the chair Schmidt sat in when he was shot.

A tongue-twister that is also a rhyming orgy:

> Did dandy Sandy bandy handy brandy candy, Randy?

**Hypozeuxis**   hī poh ZŌOK sis   (Gr. "subjoining").

Hypozeuxis (contrary to Zeugma), when every clause hath his due verb, or when to every singular thing or sentence a due verb is joined, thus: That land prospereth where God is feared, rulers obeyed, righteousness regarded, mercy maintained, charity embraced, virtues advanced, and vices repressed. This figure is of great force, to praise or dispraise, for it doth as it were paint out every quality in his several colors.

**Hyrmos**   HEER mohs   (Gr. "series").

Hyrmos, when an unfashioned order of speech is long continued, and as it were stretched out till the end, void of all round and sweet composition, thus: Harken all you that love justice, and would have reason bear rule, in all controversies and debates, knowing how all men ought to the uttermost of their power, not having regard to men, maintain the same from time to time, against all such as would by their good will and hearts desire, &c.

**Hysterologia**   his tuhr AHL oh jee uh   (Gr. "the latter discourse").

Hysterologia, when a preposition doth not serve to his causal word, but is joined to a verb, as though it were compounded with it, thus: I ran after with as much speed as I could the thief that had undone me. Here the preposition "after" is joined to the verb "I ran," which should be put next to the noun "thief," thus: With as much speed as I could, I ran after the thief that had undone me. Another: When you were upon, I am sure, the top of the hill, you might see the City, for, When you were upon the top of the hill, I am sure you might see the City.

**Icon**   Ī kahn   (Gr. "likeness; image").

Icon, when the Image of a thing or person is painted out by comparing form with form, quality with quality, and one likeness with another. It may paint forth a ravenous and venomous person after this manner:

INCREMENTUM

Even like a crested Dragon, which with burning eyes, sharp teeth, crooked nails, gaping mouth, runneth round about, seeking everywhere whom he may find to blow out his poison upon, whom he may catch in his mouth, crash in sunder with his teeth, venom with his tongue, rend in pieces with his nails.

## Imprecatio   im pre KAHT ee oh   (L. "praying on").

Imprecatio, when we curse and detest some person or thing, for the evils that they bring with them, or for the wickedness that is in them, after this manner. Cicero: O most abominable wickedness, worthy to be buried in the bottom of the earth, woe to the workers of such wickedness.

## Incrementum   in kre MEN tum   (L. "increasing").

Incrementum, when by degrees we ascend to the top of something, or rather above the top; that is, when we make our saying grow and increase by an orderly placing of our words, making the latter word always exceed the former, contrary to the natural order of things, for that ever putteth the worthiest and weightiest words first, but this placeth them always last, thus. He contemneth money, honor, pleasures, and life, for love of his country. In this figure, order must be diligently observed, that the stronger may follow the weaker, and the worthier the less worthy; otherwise you shall not increase the Oration, but make a mingle mangle, as doth the ignorant, or else make a great heap, as doth Congeries.

## Macrologia   mak roh LOHJ ee ah   (Gr. "long discourse").

Macrologia is a superfluous addition of one word or more to the end of a construction, thus: He is alive yet, God be praised, and is not dead; He hath drunk up all, and left none; he was not then awake, but fast asleep; he was never out of England, but always in England; he was always a fool, and was never wise. It is needless to add the latter clauses, seeing that they are understood of their contraries.

**Meiosis**   mī OHS is   (Gr. "lessening").

Meiosis, contrary to Auxesis, when we use a less word for a greater, to make the matter much less than it is, as when one is wounded, to say he is scarce touched; to call a notable thief a briber; to call a liar a great speaker; a flatterer, a fairspoken man. As the other doth magnify and lift up, so this doth debase and pluck down.

**Membrum**   MEM brum   (L. "limb").

Membrum, when the oration is pronounced with three or four members, either coupled or uncoupled, thus: See what a great offence and adversity thou hast brought to thyself by one wicked deed; thou hast consumed thy inheritance, cast thy parents into sorrow, driven away thy friends, defiled thy name, and provoked God to anger. Also, So worthy a man was he, that even his enemies could not but confess that he was faithful in friendship, a performer of his promise, a Father to the Fatherless, a guide to the Widow, a Teacher to the ignorant.

**Metabasis**   me TAB uh sis   (Gr. "passing over").

Metabasis, when in a few words we show what hath been already said, and also what shall be next said, and that in divers ways. First, from the equal: The things that you have already heard were very pleasant, and those that you shall hear are no less delectable. From the unequal: I have shown you his wicked deeds, yet I will show you now far more abominable facts by him committed. From the contrary: As I have spoken of his greedy gathering together of his great substance, so will I now speak of his prodigality in spending the same. From the diverse: You heard what his learning is, now shall you hear what his manners be. From the consequents and relatives: You have been told how he promised, now I will tell you how he performed. This exornation both putteth in mind what hath been said, and also prepareth the hearer for the rest following.

**Metalepsis**   me tuh LEP sis   (Gr. "participation; alteration").

Metalepsis, when we go by degrees to that which is showed, a figure seldom used of Orators, and not oft of Poets, as to say, He lieth in a dark dungeon; now in speaking of darkness, we understand closeness; by closeness, blackness; by blackness, deepness. Virgil by ears of Corn signifieth the harvests, by harvests, summers, and by summers, years.

**Metania**   me TAN ee uh   (Gr. "repentance")

Metania comprehendeth under Correctio; and it is a description of things by reprehension, thus: He played the man among his enemies, nay he played the Lion; he did beat them sore, nay he did flay the most of them, nay every one. Also when the Orator correcteth & blameth himself. Cicero: We are fools that dare compare Drusus, Africanus, Pompeius, and ourselves with Clodius.

**Metaplasmus**   me tuh PLAZ mus   (Gr. "remolding").

Metaplasmus is a transformation of letters or syllables in single words, contrary to the common fashion of writing or speaking, either for cause of necessity, or else to make the verse more fine, under which these fourteen figures following be contained: Prothesis · Aphaeres · Epenthesis · Syncope · Paragoge · Apocope · Systole · Diastole · Ecthlipsis · Synaloepha · Synacresis · Diaresis · Antistoechon · Metathesis

**Metastasis**   me TAS tuh sis   (Gr. "changing").

Metastasis, when we turn back those things that are objected against us to them that laid them onto us. When Anthony charged Cicero that he was the cause of civil war raised between Pompeius and Caesar, Cicero did rebound the same accusation again to Anthony, saying: Thou Marcus Anthony, thou I say gavest to Caesar cause to make war against thy country (turning all upside down).

**Hobson-Jobson** HOB son JOB son
Folk-etymological alteration of a word.

English soldiers in India heard Muslims of the Shiite persuasion wailing "O Hasan, O Husain," this being a ritual cry of mourning for two grandsons of Mohammed who were slain in battle. The soldiers soon altered the cry to "Hobson-Jobson," after two English surnames. The assimilation of an Oriental expression to an English word came to be called "Hobson-Jobson," later applied to any such Englishing of a foreign word, and even to the shift of one English word into another. The origins of some Hobson-Jobsons:

> Kickshaw (fancy food): French *quelque chose,* "something."
> Forlorn hope: Dutch *verloren hoop,* "lost troop."
> Crayfish: French *crévis.*
> Toodle-oo: Perhaps from French *tout à l'heure,* "so long."
> Pinkie (the little finger): Dutch *pinkje,* "small."
> Apple-pie (order): French *nap plié,* "neatly folded linen."
> (Not give a) hoot: *hoot* corrupts *iota,* smallest of the Greek letters.
> Egg on: *Egg* assimilates *edge.*
> Curry favor: In a French satire, Favel was the king's horse; a favor-seeker would offer to "curry Favel." In English, *Favel* became *favor.*
> Shamefaced: The second part issues not from *face* but from Old English *faest,* "firm." To be shamefaced is to be held fast by shame.
> Hangnail: There is no connection with *hang;* the word corrupts Middle English *agnail,* "painful prick in the flesh."
> Sand blind (half blind): There is no connection with *sand;* the syllable corrupts the obsolete prefix *sam,* "half."

(Eat) humble pie: The *humble* has nothing to do with the familiar adjective meaning "meek, lowly"; the *humbles* were the edible organs of an animal.

Nitwit: No relationship to *nit* (a louse egg) or *wit*. It perhaps derives from Dutch *niet wit,* "I don't know."

Andiron: No connection with *iron*. It comes from Old French *andier,* "fire dog"; andirons were often decorated with heads of dogs or other animals.

The Nilsens (*Language Play*) point out that *belfry* has no relation to *bell*. It descends from Middle English *berfrey,* "portable siege tower." *Pickax* has no relation to *ax;* it is from Middle English *pikois;* since the meaning was "pickax," *ax* became part of the corrupted word. *Titmouse* has no relationship to either *tit* (nipple) or *mouse;* it is from onomatopoeic *tit* for a small animal, plus *mose,* the name of the bird. *Wormwood* has no etymologic connection with *wood* or *worm;* it corrupts *wermod,* the old name for the bitter-tasting plant. *Woodchuck* has nothing to do with either *wood* or *chuck;* it corrupts the Indian name *wuchak* or *otchock. Muskrat* is from Algonquin *musquash; rat* is a corruption. The *lounge* in *chaise lounge* is from *long: chaise longue,* "a long chair." *Helpmate* comes from not *mate,* but *meet:* "But for Adam," says Genesis 2:21, "there was not found an *help meet* for him." There is no *roar* in *uproar;* the word hobson-jobsons Middle Dutch *opreer* (*op,* "up" + *roer,* "motion"). Nor is there *rage* in *outrage;* the word is from Old French *outrer,* "to overdo." There is no *cough* in *hiccough;* the earlier and still better word was *hiccup,* an imitation from the sound of hiccuping. No *house* is involved in *penthouse;* the present word alters Middle English *pentis,* "appendage."

**Mimeisis**   mi MEE sis   (Gr. "mimic").

Mimeisis, an imitation of speech whereby we counterfeit not only what one said, but also utterance and gesture, imitating everything as it was, whether he spake with moderation coldly, or with rage hotly, whether with cutting it short, or drawing it out long; with stammering, with loud or low voice, lisping, nodding the head, winking, frowning, and other like circumstances serving to the purpose. A cunning Orator will make a wise man's tale appear very pithy and pleasant, both with his fine order of speech, and also with his comely gesture; and to hear any saying imitated handsomely doth very much delight and please the hearer. Some be so excellent in this kind of counterfeiting that they are able to make a wise man's sayings better, and a fool's much worse; and if they counterfeit a foolish man's tale, they will do it in such sort that as many as hear them shall not choose but laugh, and that heartily.

**Mycterismus**   mik tor IZ mus   (Gr. "turning up the nose").

Mycterismus, a counterfeit scoffing and manner of jesting, that it may be well perceived, thus. I pray you tell me one thing, if a statute be made that all Knaves shall be banished out of England, where will you take shipping? When the Orator casting a little Shadow & color upon his speech, doth prettily and privily taunt some man's vices, and as it were glance with frumping bolts at follies, it is said by this figure.

**Obtestatio**   ob tes TAHT ee oh   (L. "calling as a witness; supplication").

Obtestatio, when we seek by prayer to get favor, or to obtain that which we would fain have, thus. Terence: Chremes I beseech thee for God's sake, and for our old friendship, which hath continued ever since we were children, which time hath also increased, and for thy only daughter's sake, & my son's sake, whom I have committed wholly to thy government, help me in this matter. Paul to the Romans 12: I beseech you brethren by the mercifulness of God, that you make your bodies a quick sacrifice, &c.

**Ominatio**   oh mi NAHT ee oh   (L. "omen").

Ominatio, when we do show & foretell what shall hereafter come to pass, which we gather by some likely sign, and in ill things we foretell it, to the intent that heed may be paid, and the danger avoided; and in good things to stir up expectation and hope. Cicero against Anthony: If thou followest these counsels, believe me, thou canst not long continue. Virgil to Turnus: Time shall come when this prodigality will be turned to poverty, and this bravery to beggary, for so we may say when we see one that is without lands spend more in a day than he getteth in a month.

**Optatio**   op TAHT ee oh   (L. "wishing").

Optatio, when we wish unto God for the maintenance of goodness and redress of evil, in whose power it only dependeth, or thus, when we wish for that we would gladly have, after this manner. Cicero: I would the immortal Gods had granted that we might rather have given thanks to Serpius Sulpititius being alive, than now to examine his honors being dead.

**Ordinatio**   or di NAHT ee oh   (L. "order").

Ordinatio, a figure which doth not only number the parts before they be said, but also doth order those parts, and maketh them plain by a kind of definition, thus. There be three things which men do greedily covet, riches, pleasures, and honors. Riches be the source of sin and iniquity, pleasure is the daughter of dishonesty, and the guide that leadeth to calamity; honors are the mother of worldly pomp and vanity.

**Parabola**   pa RAB oh lah   (Gr. "juxtaposition").

Parabola is a similitude taken of those things which are done, or of those which are joined to things by nature or hap. A ship hoisting up, taking down, or winding his sails on this side or that side is a parable teaching a wise man to give place to times, and to accommodate and bend

**PARADIASTOLE**

himself to things present. The holy Scriptures are plentiful of parables, and especially the Gospels, as: The Sower went out to sow his seed, &c. A king made a marriage for his Son, &c. Now because they be common, I need not give any more examples.

**Paradiastole**   pa ra dī AS toh lee   (Gr. "putting together of dissimilar things").

Paradiastole, nigh kin to Meiosis; and it is when by a mannerly interpretation we do excuse our own vices, or other men's whom we do defend, by calling them virtues, as when we call him that is crafty, wise; a covetous man, a good husband; murder, a manly deed; deep dissimulation, singular wisdom; covetousness, a necessary carefulness; whoredom, youthful delight & dalliance; idolatry, pure religion; gluttony and drunkenness, good fellowship; cruelty, severity. This figure is used when vices are excused.

**Paradigma**   pa ra DIG muh   (Gr. "comparing; exhibiting").

Paradigma is the rehearsal of a deed or saying past, and applying it to our purpose. The holy Scriptures have true examples of all sorts, which do manifestly show us how God hath punished pride, covetousness, drunkenness, gluttony, whoredom, Ambition, perjury, unfaithfulness, and all other manner of sins, how he hath destroyed the ungodly, and exalted the lovers of his laws.

Feigned examples are taken from Poets' inventions, and fables attributed to brute creatures, as to beasts, birds, fowls, fishes, and also to trees, rivers, Mountains. This kind bringeth a great delectation to his hearers, but especially to the Simple sort, who delight a great deal more to hear fond fables than grave matters; yet being aptly applied, they also delight the wise and learned, and have been always by learned men well allowed and liked of.

**Paragoge**   pa ra GOHJ ee   (Gr. "protracting").

Paragoge is the addition of a letter or syllable to the end of a word, as: "Yet never seen beforn" for "before"; "Now hasten well your work" for "haste"; "She gazeth at the strangy sight" for "strange."

**Paramologia**   pa ra moh LOHJ ee uh   (Gr. "partial admission").

Paramologia, when we grant many things to our adversaries, and at the last bring in one thing that overthroweth all that were granted before, thus. Cicero for Flaccus: Notwithstanding this I say, concerning the whole nation of the Greeks, I grant them learning, I grant them the knowledge of many arts; I take not from them the comely grace of speech, fine wits, singular eloquence; yet religion and faith that nation hath never favored nor loved; what virtue, what authority, what weight there is of all this matter they know not.

**Paregmenon**   pa REG muh non   (Gr. "leading aside; changing").

Paregmenon, when of the word going before the word following is derived, thus. It was a marvel most marvelous, and a wonder most wonderful. Paul to the Romans 9: Let him that exhorteth give attendance to his exhortation. And likewise when the word following is the same that goeth before. Thus, Paul: Be merry with them that be merry, weep also with them that weep.

**Parelcon**   pa REL kon   (Gr. "drawing aside or along; spinning out").

Parelcon, when a syllable is added to the end of a word, or when two words are joined together in one, thus: forwhy I could not otherwise do; whenthat I call, I pray ye be ready; whywhat is the matter; forif it could have been, it should have been. In the first clause "for" had been sufficient, in the second "when," in the third "what," and in the fourth "if," without the addition of the others.

**Parenthesis**   pa REN thuh sis   (Gr. "inserting").

Parenthesis, when a sentence is set asunder by the interposition of another, or when a sense is cast between the speech, before it be all ended, which although it give some strength, yet when it is taken away, it leave the same speech perfect enough, thus. Virgil: To her again (for well she knew she spake with feigned mind) then Venus answered thus . . .

**Paroemia**   pa REEM ee uh   (Gr. "proverb").

Paroemia, a saying much used, and commonly known, and also very excellent for the Novelty; to which two things are required; one that it be notable, renowned, and much spoken of, a sentence in every man's mouth, called of the Latins an adage, and of us Englishmen, a proverb; the other that it be pretty, feat, and witty; that is to say: that it may be discerned, by some note and mark, from common speech, and also commended by antiquity, and learning.

Terence: I hold the Wolf by the ears, by which is signified that that is both dangerous to hold, and also to let go. All our English proverbs be of this Figure, as, You hit the nail on the head; all the Fat is in the fire; the blind drink many a fly; you trust to a broken staff; the burnt child doth fear the fire.

**Paroemion**   pa REEM ee ahn   (Gr. "like letters").

Paroemion, when many words beginning with one letter are set in one sentence, thus: This mischievous Money makes many men marvelous mad; When friendly favor flourished, I found felicity; she walked and wandered out of the way, weeping and wailing upon her woeful wound. This differeth from Cacemphaton, for that beginneth with like syllables, but this with the same letter.*

*Paroemion = alliteratio. (See p. 44.)

**What's the question?**

In this parlor game, said to have been popular at the White House during the presidency of John F. Kennedy, an answer is given and the players are supposed to deduce from it what the question was—which is usually impossible, as you will agree after a look at the samples below.

*Answers:*

1. A youthful figure.
2. Black.
3. Strontium 90, Carbon 14.
4. Around the world in eighty days.
5. George Washington slept here.
6. From the rock-bound coast of Maine.
7. Stork Club.

*Questions:*

1. What do you get when you ask a woman her age?
2. What color is a board of education?
3. What was the final score of the Strontium-Carbon game?
4. What was the slogan of that airline that went out of business?
5. What are all these cherry pits doing in my bed?
6. Where the hell did all these rocks come from?
7. What do you use to beat up a stork?

**Parrhesia**   pa REEZ ee uh   (Gr. "free-speaking").

Parrhesia, when speaking before them whom we ought to reverence and fear, & having something to say which either toucheth themselves or their friends, we do desire them to pardon our boldness, showing that it were great pity if for lack of admonition, vices should be maintained & virtues oppressed. Now in this figure great wariness must be used, lest too much boldness bring offence. Cicero: I speak with great peril, I fear, Judges, after what sort you will take my words. But for my continual desire that I have to retain and augment your dignity, I pray and beseech you that if my speech be either bitter or incredible unto you at the first hearing, yet that you would accept it without offence, neither that you will reject it before I have plainly opened it unto you.

**Partitio**   par TIT ee oh   (L. "dividing").

Partitio, when the whole is divided into parts, as if you might say, He is well seen in all Sciences. This general saying you may declare by parts, thus: He perfectly knoweth all the painful rules of Grammar, the pleasant flowers of Rhetoric, the subtleties of Logicians, the secrets of natural Philosophy, the difficulty of Wisdom supernatural, the pleasant Fables of Poets, the Mathematical demonstrations, the motions of Stars, the cunning reasons of numbers, the description of the world, the measuring of the earth, the situations, names, distances of Countries, Cities, Mountains, Rivers, Fountains, and Wildernesses, the properties of Soils, the deep mystery of Divinity, the difference of harmonies, the content of tunes, histories old and new, antiquities, novelties, Greek, Latin, and Hebrew.

**Pathopeia**   pa thoh PEE uh   (Gr. "making suffer").

Pathopeia, when the Orator moveth the minds of his hearers either to indignation, anger, fear, envy, hatred, hope, gladness, mirth, laughter, sorrow, or sadness. Of this there be two kinds. The first is when the Orator being moved with any of these affections (except sorrow) doth apply and bend his speech to stir his hearers to the same; and this kind is called Imagination. Matters that fall into this figure ought to be great, cruel, horrible, marvelous, and such like, as may cause the affections to flame: examples hereof be common in Tragedies. The other is when the Orator by lamenting some pitiful case maketh his hearers to weep, and also moveth them to pity, and mercy, & to pardon offenses. In this figure a pitiful pronunciation is of great force.

**Periergia**   per i ERJ ee uh   (Gr. "overcareful").

Periergia, when in a small matter there is too much labor bestowed, and too many words and figures used, and they take greater care to paint their speech with fine figures than to express the truth plainly. Some are so affectioned to figures and foolish signs that by their good wills they will not utter one sentence without a figure, and sometimes with all one figure, which giveth cause for wise men to suspect that such are prouder of their Eloquence than diligent to set forth matters with plainness.

**Perissologia**   per i soh LOHJ ee uh   (Gr. "excessive words").

Perissologia, like unto Pleonasmus, when a clause of no weight is thrust into a construction. Quintilian taketh this example out of Livius: The Ambassadors, peace not being obtained, returned home again from whence they came. Here the latter clause is superfluous, for it had been sufficient to have said, The Ambassadors, peace not being obtained, returned home again.

**Peristasis**   per IS tuh sis   (Gr. "circumstances; situation").

Peristasis, when we amplify by circumstances; and circumstances are either of a person, or of a thing. A person hath Parentage, Nation, Country, Kind, Age, Education, Discipline, Habit of body, Fortune, Condition, the nature of the mind, study, foredeeds, and name, &c. Examples. Parentage: Thou art of a noble blood, and has thou made thyself a companion of Rascals? Nation: Is it not a shame for thee, being an Englishman born, to despise the feat of shooting? Country: To be born and bred in

Middlesex, and to speak ill English, is a foul fault. Kind: For a Woman to use filthy talk is much uncomely, and a foul sight to see a man weep for a blow on the ear.

**Polisyndeton**   pah li SIN duh tahn   (Gr. "having many connections").

Polisyndeton, when a sentence is knit together with many conjunctions, contrary to Asyndeton. Cicero: We cease not both to exhort and to pray, and now boldly to blame and admonish Pompeius, that he should fly to so great an infamy.

**Pragmatographia**   prag ma toh GRAF ee uh   (Gr. "concrete description").

Pragmatographia, like unto Icon, a description of things, whereby we do as plainly describe anything by gathering together all the circumstances belonging unto it, as if it were most lively painted out in colors, and set forth to be seen. As if one should say, The City was overcome by assault; he compriseth all in a sum. But if, as sayeth Fabius, thou wilt open and set abroad those things which were included within one word, there shall appear many fires and scattered flames upon houses and temples, the noise of houses falling down, one sound of divers things & cries; some fly with great danger, others hang on their friends to bid them farewell forever; the shrieking of Infants, women weeping most bitterly, old men kept by most unhappy destiny to see that day, the spoiling of temporal and hallowed things, the running out of them that carried away spoils, and of them that entreated for their own goods; every man led chained before his spoiler; the mother wrestling and trying to hold her suckling babe; and wherever there were great riches, there was great fighting among the spoilers. Now although this word Destruction might well comprise all these things, yet it is less to declare the whole than to name everything severally.

**Preteritio**    pre tur IT ee oh    (L. "a passing over").

Preteritio, like unto Apophasis, when we make as though we would say nothing in some matter, when notwithstanding we speak most of all; or when we say something, in saying we will not say it. Cicero against Verres: I will make no mention of his drunken banquets nightly, and his watchings with Bawds, Dicers, Whoremasters; I will not name his losses, luxuriance, and disdaining of his honesty.

**Procatalepsis**    proh kat uh LEP sis    (Gr. "anticipation").

Procatalepsis, when perceiving beforehand what might be objected to against us and hurt us, we wipe it away ere ever it be spoken, or thus, when we put forth the same objection against our fellows that we think our adversaries would, and then confute it by reason. Romans 9: Thou wilt say then unto me, why then blameth he us yet, for who hath been able to resist his will? but O man, who art thou, that disputeth with God?

**Prolepsis**    proh LEP sis    (Gr. "taking beforehand").

Prolepsis, when a general word going before is afterwards divided into parts: We were both in great sorrow, I for the loss of my dear friend, and he for fear of banishment; Three Singers did sing, the Eldest the Bass, the middlemost the Mean, and the youngest the Treble, for, Three singers did sing; the Eldest did sing the Bass, the Middlemost did sing the Mean, and the Youngest did sing the Treble.

**Propositio**    proh poh ZIT ee oh    (L. "proposing").

Propositio, which compriseth in few words the sum of that matter whereof we intend to speak. Cicero against Catiline: and because the decree of the Senate is not yet written, I will show you as much thereof as I can call to remembrance.

PRETERITIO

**Prosographia**   pro soh GRAF ee uh   (Gr. "writing on").

Prosographia, like also unto Icon, when the person of an actual man is by his form, stature, manners, studies, doings, affections, and such other circumstances serving the purpose, so described that it may appear a plain picture painted in Tables, and set before the eyes of the hearer. For the plainer instruction of the unlearned, I will show how the circumstances are used in this figure. Age: An old man crooked, gray headed, his skin wrinkled, his eyes hollow, his sight dim, his hearing thick, his strength feeble; weak of memory, doting in fantasies, testy, covetous, &c. Habit of body: A tall and slender young man, very fair of complexion, grave eyed, yellow haired, in a Doublet of green Satin, hose of scarlet, a black Velvet Cap with a fair white feather, a beautiful and rich chain about his neck, fair rings of his hand, &c.

**Prothesis**   PROH thuh sis   (Gr. "putting before").

Prothesis is an addition of a letter or syllable to the beginning of a word, as: "There I am well beknown" for "known"; "This irksome love aslake" for "slake"; "Ymade to burn outright" for "made"; "Adown to the ground we fall" for "down"; "I do beweep my woe" for "weep."

**Pysma**   PEES muh   (Gr. "question").

Pysma, when we ask often times together, and use many questions in one place, whereby we do make the Oration sharp & vehement; and it differeth from Erotema, or Interrogation, for as much as interrogation may well be answered with one word, either granting or denying, but not this without many. Cicero for Roscius: In what place did he speak with them, with whom did he speak; how did he persuade them; did he hire them; whom did he hire; by whom did he hire them; to what end or how much did he give them? Now thus many questions together, are as it were like unto a courageous fighter, that doth lay strokes upon his enemy so thick and so hard that he is not able to defend or bear half of them.

**Restrictio**   re STRIKT ee oh   (L. "binding back tight").

Restrictio, when of the general word going before, a part is excepted. Paul to the Corinthians 4: We are afflicted on every side, yet are we not in distress; we are in poverty, but not overcome of poverty; we are persecuted, but not forsaken; we are cast down, yet we perish not.

**Scesisonomaton**   se si soh NAHM uh tahn   (Gr. "relation of words")

Scesisonomaton, when a sentence or saying doth consist altogether of nouns, yet when to every Substantive an Adjective is joined, thus: A man faithful in friendship, prudent in counsels, virtuous in conversation, gentle in communication, learned in all liberal sciences, eloquent in utterance, comely in gesture, pitiful to the poor, an enemy to naughtiness, a lover of all virtue & godliness.

**Sermocinatio**   ser moh si NAHT ee oh   (L. "discourse").

Sermocinatio, very like to Prosopopoeia. When the person which we feign speaketh all himself, then is it Prosopopoeia; but when we answer now and then to the question which he putteth unto us, it is called Sermocinatio. In this figure wisdom and wariness must be used that the speech be not otherwise than is likely the same person would use; otherwise our speech shall seem foolish and absurd. Therefore in this place it behooveth us diligently to consider the circumstances both of persons and things—what is their estate, condition, kind, age, disposition, manners, studies, affection, fortune, cause, place, time, and such like; for one manner of speech doth become men, and another is decent for women; children's talk is not so seasoned with reason as old men's is. Cicero in this behalf evermore gave meet speech to the person whom he feigned to speak, whether he were his adversary or his friend. He brought in Milo speaking valiantly; Anthony arrogantly; Nevius wickedly; Erutius impudently—ever framing their speech according to their nature.

**Acronym**   AK ro nim   (Gr. "outer end" + "word").
A word formed from the initial letters of a name, as ERA for Equal
Rights Amendment; or by combining parts of a series of words, as
*radar* for "*ra*dio *d*etecting *a*nd *r*anging."

According to the Census Bureau, a *P*erson *O*f *O*pposite *S*ex,
*S*haring *L*iving *Q*uarters, is a POOSSL-Q (or POSSL-Q). The
acronym for the *O*rganization of *O*il *P*roducing *S*tates is OOPS;
for *F*abbricato *I*talia *A*utomobilia *T*orino, it is FIAT. A few of the
other acronyms littering our language:

| | |
|---|---|
| AAAS | Association for the Advancement of Science |
| AD | Anno Domini (Year of Our Lord) |
| AFL–CIO | American Federation of Labor–Congress of Industrial Organizations |
| AP | Associated Press |
| AWOL | Absent Without Official Leave |
| CIA | Central Intelligence Agency |
| COD | Cash (or Collect) On Delivery |
| DST | Daylight Saving Time |
| FBI | Federal Bureau of Investigation |
| FOB | Free On Board |
| IOU | I Owe You |
| IQ | Intelligence Quotient |
| KO | Knock Out |

**Soroesmus**   soh REES mus   (Gr. "accumulation").

Soroesmus, a mingling together of divers Languages, as when there is in one sentence English, Latin & French. Some think we speak but little English, and that our speech is for the most part borrowed of other languages, but chiefly of the Latin, as to the Learned it is well known.*

**Syllogismus**   si loh JIZ mus   (Gr. "reasoning").

Syllogismus, when we amplify a matter by conjecture taken of some figure or circumstance, as to say, It rained forty days and forty nights continually, whereby it is gathered that there followed mighty floods. Virgil, speaking of one Poliphemus, sayeth: He held a Pine Tree in hand, and walked through the Sea; by this we conjecture what a great body he had, having a Pine Tree for his staff.

**Symploce**   SIM ploh see   (Gr. "an interweaving").

Symploce, when many members following have the same beginning and the same end, comprising both Epanaphora, and also Epiphora, thus. Who were they that often broke their leagues? The Carthaginians. Who were they that made cruel war in Italy? The Carthaginians. Who defaced all Italy? The Carthaginians. Who crave pardon now? The Carthaginians. This figure is more pleasant, if every repetition following have one word more than the repetition going before, thus. Remember Sodom and Gomorrah; remember the sin of Sodom and Gomorrah; remember the sin and destruction of Sodom and Gomorrah.

**Synaeresis**   si NEER uh sis   (Gr. "taking or drawing together; contracting").

Synaeresis, when of two syllables in measuring, there is made but one, as when of the word virtuous, which hath three syllables, we pronounce it with but two, thus virtues, and also esteem'd for esteemèd.

---

*Soroesmus is familiar in present-day English under the name macaronics.

SYNCHORESIS

**Synaloepha**   si na LEEF uh   (Gr. "smearing or melting together").

Synaloepha, when two vowels come together, and the first of them is cut off, as: "Th' Arcadians' guise was this" for "The Arcadians"; "Show me no more; I see't" for "see it"; "I came t'ask indeed this thing" for "to ask."

**Synchisis**   SIN ki sis   (Gr. "mingling; confusing").

Synchisis, a confusion of order, in all parts of the construction. Virgil: The wines good which afterward had in pipes laid aboard Acestes, and given to the Trojans departing, the noble man did distribute. This saying is so darkened by confusion of order that it is almost impossible to be understood, for the plain order placeth it thus: The noble man did afterward distribute the wines which good Acestes, king of Sicily, had laid aboard and given to the departing Trojans. Of this figure there need be no more examples, for that it is unprofitable, and rather to be avoided than at any time to be imitated.

**Synchoresis**   sin KOR uh sis   (Gr. "going along").

Synchoresis, when trusting strongly to our cause, we give the Judges or our adversaries leave to consider and judge of it, according to their discretion. Cicero: But now, Judges, I leave the whole and most lawful right of my cause which I have declared, and commit it unto you to determine of it as you shall think most reasonable. Here Cicero by yielding up his whole cause into the Judges' hands doth move them very much to favor it, for thereby he declared that he had a good opinion and trust that their dealing therein would be upright and just, which must needs cause the Judges to deal rather favorably than severely.

**Synonimia**   si noh NIM ee uh   (Gr. "same name").

Synonimia, when by a variation and change of words that be of like signification we iterate one thing divers times. Virgil: How doth the child Ascanius, and is he yet alive? Doth he eat ethereal food? and lieth he not yet below among the cruel shades? Here he demandeth nothing else but whether Ascanius be alive or not, yet through affection he expresseth one thing thrice. Sometimes with words, thus: Alas many woes, cares, sorrows, troubles, calamities, berations, and miseries do besiege me round about.

**Systole**   SIS toh lee   (Gr. "contraction").

Systole, when a long Syllable is made short, contrary to the nature thereof. *Da*rius for *Da*rius, *Di*ana for Dia*n*a, *Jo*sephus for Jo*seph*us.

**Tapinosis**   ta pi NOHS is   (Gr. "lowering").

Tapinosis, when the majesty of a high matter is brought down and much defaced by the baseness of a word, as to call the Ocean Sea a stream, a Lady's Couch a Cart, a Musician a fiddler, a Castle an house, an Oration a tale, a foughten field a fray, eloquence babbling; evermore when a low word is applied to signify a high matter, the same is Tapinosis.

**Tautologia**   tah toh LOHJ ee uh   (Gr. "same word").

Tautologia, an unprofitable and irksome repetition of one word, or matter, which happen commonly to them that sing always one song, thus. If you have a friend, I would be with you to keep a friend, for an old friend is to be preferred before a new friend; if I were your friend, I would never take you again for my friend if you should once forsake me your old friend and take a new friend. This is contrary to Exposition, a virtue which repeateth one thing divers ways, with pleasant variety.

**Taxis**   TAK sis   (Gr. "arrangement; order").

Taxis, much like to Hypozeuxis, when everything is evidently distinguished with new Verbs, thus. To inveigh against their vices it was unlawful to keep silence, it was not expedient to speak suspiciously, it was best accepted. Cicero: By this means, our Ancestors first conquered all Italy; then cast down Carthage, overthrew Numance, and brought most mighty Kings, and most valiant Nations, to the dominion of the Empire.

**Tophothesia**   toh foh THEEZ ee uh   (Gr. "description of a place").

Tophothesia, a feigned description of a place; that is, when we describe a place, and yet there is no such place, as the house of Envy in the first book of Metamorphosis, the house of Sleep in the seventh book; or else it is not such a place as it is feigned to be, as is Heaven and Hell in the fourth book of Eneidos. This Figure is proper to Poets, and seldom used of Orators.

**Topographia**   tah poh GRAF ee uh   (Gr. "describing places").

Topographia, an evident and true description of a place. To this Figure refers Cosmography, by which is described Countries, Cities, Towns, Temples, Walls, Gates, Buildings, Mountains, Rivers, Fountains, Fields, Orchards, Gardens, and any other manner of places.

**Traductio**   tra DOOK tee oh   (L. "a transferring").

Traductio, like unto Tautologia, when one word is sundry times repeated in one sentence, to make the Oration more trim, thus: Let riches belong to rich men, but prefer thou virtue before riches, for if thou wilt compare riches with virtue, thou shalt think riches scarce meet to be handmaidens to virtue. Daniel 2: O king thou art a King of kings. This figure the poets call Polyploton.

# PRONUNCIATION GUIDE

| | | | |
|---|---|---|---|
| a | cat | m | more |
| ay | pay | n | now |
| ah | father | oh | go |
| aw | jaw | oo | boot |
| b | bug | ow | how |
| k | catch | oy | toy |
| ch | chew | p | pill |
| d | do | r | red |
| e | let | s | so |
| ee | seem | sh | sure |
| f | fun | t | tall |
| g | get | th | thin |
| h | heavy | u | must |
| i | it | uh | abut |
| ī | sky | v | very |
| j | jam | w | well |
| k | king | y | yes |
| ks | sex | z | zero |
| kw | quill | zh | vision |
| l | love | | |

# BIBLIOGRAPHY

*The American Heritage Dictionary,* 1978
*A Dictionary of Contemporary American Usage,* Bergen and Cornelia Evans
*The Garden of Eloquence,* Henry Peacham
*Language Play,* Don L. F. and Alleen Pace Nilson
*Modern American Usage,* Wilson Follett
*Modern English Usage,* W. H. Fowler
*The New Revised Encyclopaedic Dictionary,* 1896
*The Oxford English Dictionary,* 1969
*Power Writing, Power Speaking,* N. H., S. K., P. S. Mager
*Webster's New International Dictionary of the English Language,* Second Edition, Unabridged, 1961

# INDEX OF FIRST LINES OF
# W.R.E. VERSES

*(First lines of verses that appeared in previous Espy books are marked with an asterisk.)*

# INDEX OF FIGURES OF SPEECH

# ABOUT THE AUTHOR

Willard Espy's interest in words turned professional in the mid-1960s, when he submitted some verses he had written for fun to the English magazine *Punch*. The magazine not only accepted the anagrams, but for several years published a weekly verse by Espy. These were subsequently published in book form, in England and the United States, as *The Game of Words*. Since that time, Willard Espy has published many books on language, including *An Almanac of Words at Play; O Thou Improper, Thou Uncommon Noun;* and *Say It My Way*. Mr. Espy has written for numerous newspapers and magazines, and has appeared often on radio and television. He and his wife Louise spend half their time in New York City, and half in Oysterville, Washington.